COASTAL
ESSEX

───── ROBERT SIMPER ─────

COASTAL ESSEX

Published by Creekside Publishing 2011
www.creeksidepublishing.co.uk

ISBN: 978-0-9563299-1-2
COPYRIGHT Robert Simper

Printed by The Lavenham Press

Front Cover. The Colne barge and smack race, 2006.
Frontispiece. Swans on the River Stour with smack *Daisy Belle* on her mooring.
Back cover. Smacks on their moorings, in the Besom, West Mersea.

EAST ANGLIAN BOOKS

Over Snape Bridge (1967)
Woodbridge & Beyond (1972)
Suffolk Show (1981)
East Anglian Coast & Waterways (1985)
Suffolk Sandlings (1986)
Woodbridge: Pictorial History (1995)
Suffolk: A Fine Farming County (2007)
Woodbridge to the Coast (2008)
Coastal Suffolk (2009)

SAIL BOOKS

East Coast Sail (1972)
Scottish Sail (1974)
North East Sail (1975)
British Sail (1977)
Victorian & Edwardian Yachting from Old Photographs (1978)
Gaff Sail (1979)
Sail on the Orwell (1982)
Sail: The Surviving Tradition (1984)

BRITISH ISLES

Britain's Maritime Heritage (1982)
Beach Boats of Britain (1984)

ENGLISH ESTUARIES SERIES

The Deben River (1992)
The River Orwell and the River Stour (1993)
Rivers Alde, Ore and Blyth (1994)
Essex Rivers and Creeks (1995)
Norfolk Rivers and Harbours (1996)
Thames Tideway (1997)
River Medway and The Swale (1998)
Rivers to the Fens (2000)
Up the River Deben (2006)

AUTOBIOGRAPHICAL

In Search of Sail (1998)
Family Fields (1999)
Voyage Around East Anglia (2001)
Creekside Tales (2004)

COAST IN THE PAST SERIES

Forgotten Coast (2002)   British Isles
Sunrise Coast (2002)   Suffolk & N.Essex
The Lugger Coast (2003) Cornwall & Devon
The Barge Coast of Suffolk, Essex and Kent (2007)

CONTENTS

Chapter Four

THE MIGHTY BLACKWATER

West Mersea around to Bradwell

Chapter Five

THE ESTUARY COAST

Rivers Crouch, Roach Islands and Thames Mouth

INTRODUCTION

The Essex coast has certainly not passed unrecorded, but this lively county moves forward at speed and this is my attempt to chronicle the situation so far. There was a long pioneering period from medieval times to the nineteenth century when the coast was the frontier and the river walls were built. Essex rivers were commercial highways from the earliest time, but in the nineteenth and early twentieth centuries the barge traffic reached its peak. At the same time fishing and oysters were also at their peak. As the barge era declined the estuaries became almost deserted until mass-produced fibreglass yachts appeared in the 1960s and leisure boating re-shaped these coastal regimes and brought life back to the waterfronts.

The low-lying coast of Essex, with its wide-open skies towering above, is a land of tremendous contrasts. The cheerful beach resorts of Clacton and Southend are totally different places to the forty or so marsh islands. Then there are open estuaries lined with innumerable creeks and thousands of acres of grey mud. If you don't like mud, you probably don't like the Essex estuaries.

The Essex coast forms the northern shore of the Thames Estuary. The Environment Agency have stated that Essex has over '440 miles of coast', but most of these riverside marshes are easy to defend and there are only about 30 miles of open coast facing the Thames Estuary. The Essex marshlands were left to those few people who lived and worked there. The visitors are occasional yachtsmen, walkers and bird watchers. Although the great Essex wilderness of mud and marsh remains isolated, it has been thrust into the political spotlight. The Essex coastal marshlands became a battleground between highly productive agriculture and the bird empires, really highlighting the tremendous pressure there is on land space in south-east England.

In 1992 the UK signed the European Union Habitat Directive, that became statute in 1994. The Directive requires the UK Government to protect all EU designated habitat in situ. In about 1998 Defra's environmental strategists concluded that it would be cheaper to relocate the habitat sites inland rather than protect the coast.

When Global Warming became recognised, the Government gave grants to professors to say exactly what was going to happen and some alarming predictions began to be made about a rapid rise in sea levels. The Government was seriously worried and decided to quietly abandon the English coast and let everyone move inland on to higher ground. This policy, which was not really brought to the public's attention, will, if it continues, have a devastating effect on the coastal communities of the United Kingdom. The Government has attempted to keep sea defences on the town fronts, but when the land on either side erodes away these really will become unsustainable. The Government failed to take into account that England is already over populated. Unlike California in the 1870s there are no empty valleys in England waiting to be populated. As people are forced to move inland and new towns are built it will prove much more disruptive socially than the closing of the coalmines.

Land space and fresh water are the most valuable assets any nation has, and this is fully realized just across the North Sea by the Dutch. The Netherlands, a country of only 17m population, has far greater problems than the UK, but they quietly get on with dealing with a rising sea level. Walls are steadily made higher, often with soil dredged off the English coast, and land drainage pumps are made more powerful.

Unfortunately, in the UK the Government agencies have become impregnated by a kind of defeatist attitude. Defeatism has been institutionalised first with Managed Retreat and then with the Make Space for Water policy.

No-one in UK Government agencies seems to have been much bothered by the effect of the sea pushing people inland, but it suddenly dawned on the agencies that the EU agreement meant that the UK had to protect 192 sites of natural habitat on the coast, covering some 32,000h (79,040 acres). Defra insisted that they would still let the sea move inland, which would destroy bird habitat, but they would have to take money away from coastal defences and use these funds to 'relocate' bird habitat inland. This is a double damage policy. With funds taken away from coastal defences erosion speeds up, and particularly in Essex, flooding with salt water is destroying increasing amounts of important fresh water wildlife habitat, which cannot be replaced.

In 2006 it was realised that the alarmist predictions about sea level rise acceleration were, to date, exaggerated. The sea was still slightly rising, exactly as it has done for at least the last four hundred years. Far from Global Warming producing more storm surges, the records show that on the East Anglian coast between 1964 and 2010 the number of tidal surges fell in height and frequency. This does not mean that the 1953 size tidal surge couldn't happen next winter, just that it is extremely unlikely. History has shown that about once every hundred years there has been, usually totally unexpectedly, a storm surge that has flooded towns and land. This will continue, but afterwards people can return, as they have done before, to resume living there.

The Government should have returned to a proper policy of defending the coast, but Defra had got the bit between its teeth and ploughed manfully on with its plan to flood much of Coastal Essex, telling the public that they had to do it because of the EU agreement and accelerating sea levels, when exactly the opposite was true. There certainly is not an EU quota of land that has to be flooded each year; this is something that appears to have been invented in the UK. Defra seems to have been the source of a highly organized campaign, with colour photographs, glamorising the flooding of land. Local people were 'consulted' for their views, but if these views didn't follow the Managed Retreat Policy they were often ridiculed. Part of this campaign is to claim that the centuries old river walls (they are actually part of the heritage of the area) are 'worn out.'

The old 'wallers' used to walk along the saltings and if they could see over the river walls they knew that the walls needed heightening. This was mostly due to wall settlement and sea level rise increasing the height of saltings, a combined total of about 0.8m(2.6 feet per century.) The 'wallers' then dug the soil out of the salting with shovels and made the walls higher. This was good because the holes in the saltings filled up with silt coming in from the sea. The system worked well for over five hundred years and, if you could find anyone with a shovel, this system would still go on working. There is no problem with maintaining the river walls, with mechanisation it is actually a simple operation. The danger is not entirely from the sea, it is muddled thinking on the landward side that is often causing the damage.

The one thing that the Essex coast is not short of is foreshore habitat for birds, there are thousands of acres of it, but it is a good idea to try and preserve some saltings in danger. This can be done by putting facing to protect them from the wave action and shore crabs, which is a great deal cheaper that the cost of flooding marshes. The Essex marshlands are a highly fragile environment, only just held together for centuries by sheer hard work. Flooding land increases the tidal flow in the rivers and runs a high risk of destabilising the whole area. With Government agencies totally fixated on 'managed realignment' no consideration of any sort is given to the side effects of their flooding policy. The increased water flow in the estuaries speeds up erosion.

Instead of coming up with a plan to defend the coast the Government agencies are grimly plugging on with determination with their policy of flooding and destroying as much as possible. It is a nightmare situation because the Essex coast is highly fragile; there are enough problems with erosion without helping the sea to eat more land. As things stand the people, land and heritage are under serious threat in coastal Essex and for that matter in much of south east England.

ACKNOWLEDGEMENTS

The man who really understood coastal Essex was Hervey Benham. He was really the first to realize that the workboats of the coast were an integral part of its heritage. Hervey's books, particularly 'Down Tops'l,' inspired my generation. Many people have helped me in my researches on coastal Essex. On Mistley's shipping Roy Fenton, Richard Titchener were informative and also Nick Temple talked about the Stour lighter he has steered into being rebuilt. Chris Byford Smith, third generation Kirby man, told me about Walton Backwaters and Hugh Perks researched the Clacton barges. On Brightlingsea and St Osyth Malcolm 'Mac' Macgregor and Dick Harman reminisced about their early days in fishing. Thanks to Trazar Astley Reid for information on the Essex river walls. Nick Baker was informative on Rowhedge waterfront. Russell Large recalled his seventeen happy years on Osea. On sailing barges, Barry Pearce of Maldon has patiently answered many questions and passed on information that Mark Hicks of Mistley had told him fifty years earlier. Other information on Maldon was drawn from John Rogers and Stephen P. Nunn. On Bradwell, thanks go to Roger Beckett and Kevin Bruce of Tillingham. Richard Welsh on North Fambridge and help came from Robin Nicholls on Great Wakering. Nicki Uden and Bob Crumb on Foulness. Steve Hall supplied material on Tollesbury and Leigh. On Leigh fishing, Trevor Osborne, Paul Gilson and 'Brom' Bromley passed on their knowledge. Above all Richard Stewart has explained to me mysteries of the tide line, showing the destructive work of crabs and passing on information about the sea's behaviour.

Janet Harker has drawn excellent free-hand maps of the coast she loves so dearly. Unfortunately names of photographers who took some of the early black and white photographs seem to have been lost in the mists of time, but Ron Nott took the photograph of the *Cap Pilar*. Jonathan Simper took the colour photograph of Fingringhoe ballast quay and Peter Baldwin took the photograph of the group of lifeboats. Most of the other colour photographs were taken by myself.

My wife Pearl has done the first editing and took the photograph of breakwater on Frinton beach and Diana McMillan helped with the final editing, many thanks to all these people.

RS. Ramsholt, 2011

Chapter One
HARWICH TO THE NAZE
Harwich Harbour, River Stour and Walton Backwaters

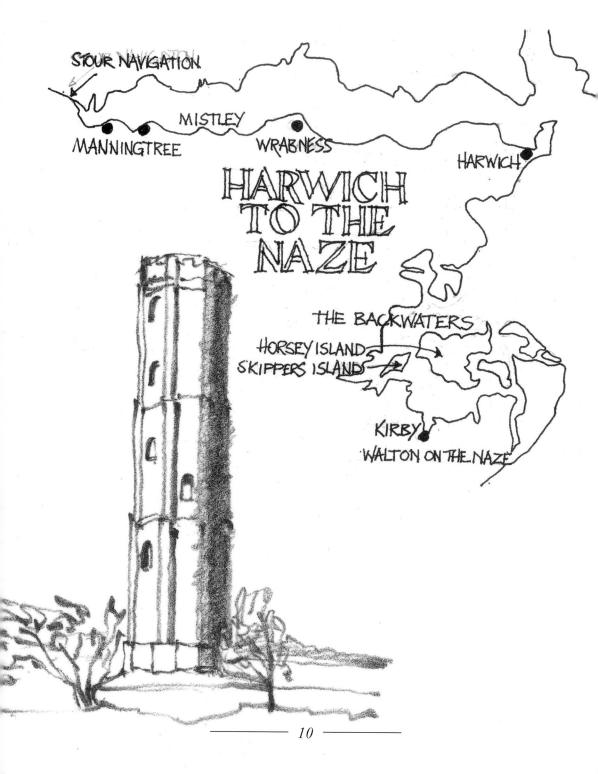

STOUR NAVIGATION

MISTLEY

MANNINGTREE   WRABNESS

HARWICH

HARWICH TO THE NAZE

THE BACKWATERS

HORSEY ISLAND
SKIPPERS ISLAND

KIRBY
WALTON ON THE NAZE

HARWICH

'Its all up at Harwich' the coastal sailors used to say about Harwich, meaning that the town was a depressed place. The little windswept town sitting on the very tip of Essex was built to serve shipping and some have said 'Harwich is all churches and pubs' to cater for the sailors' different needs ashore.

The name Harwich is thought to mean 'hare' for army and 'wic' for a camp. Which might be a place where Alfred the Great's Anglo-Saxon army camped before fighting the Danish Vikings in 885. The Vikings arrived in thirteen longships and the battle of Stourmouth is believed to have taken place across the harbour at Bloody Point. In recent years Trinity House has seen fit to drop the name Bloody Point on the buoy at the end of the spit and change it to the more polite 'Shotley Point'.

The point that Harwich and its quays were built on was called Harwich Ness and, since it had access into deep water, a Royal Dockyard was started here in 1674 to build men-of-war. The Navy gave up its dockyard at Harwich in 1827 and the Navy Yard was then used for commercial shipbuilding. Father and son Vaux built schooners, barges and Harwich cod smacks here and McLearon built and repaired sailing barges at the Navy Yard between 1895-1927, but in 1964 the whole area vanished under the commercial quay for roll-on, roll-off ferries to Europe.

In the property boom of about 2005 Harwich still had some of the lowest priced houses in England and in 2009 it was classified as being one of the most commercially endangered towns in England, as most of its shops had closed. The truth was that Harwich and Dovercourt, a Victorian seaside resort just inland, had merged into one town and the remaining shops had moved there. St Nicholas' Church dominates the middle of Harwich and can be clearly seen from Harwich Harbour. St Nicholas church was originally built of wood but was rebuilt in 1822.

When Trinity House operated pilots for the ships entering Ipswich and the Haven ports there were over a hundred pilots based at Harwich, all living within half an hour's travelling time of the pilot station. In 1988 Trinity House handed over the control of pilotage to the local port authority and the number of pilots was reduced to about thirty-five. With ships getting larger and many masters being licensed to bring in their own vessels, the number of pilots was reduced further, to about twenty-five.

MISTLEY

Mistley was a quiet village with a few fishermen and people connected with farms until Richard Rigby inherited Mistley Hall in the eighteenth century. He hired Robert Adam, the leading architect of the day, to create a new Mistley Hall and Mistley Spa, a place for the fashionable set to visit and take the waters. Rigby's Spa never really got off the ground, but his other plan, to turn Mistley into a port, worked rather well. He built quays, a dock and a shipyard and cottages for his workers to live in. A famous visitor to the Hall, the actor David Garrick, counted fifty vessels under sail on the River Stour when looking out of his dressing room window.

In 1770 Rigby opened a shipyard at the west end of Mistley. This yard launched an East Indiaman and twelve warships, the largest being the 914 ton *Amphian*. The shipyard was on Thorn Reach, above the quay, where Portishead house now stands. There had been large capstans on the green, used for hauling ships up the slipway, on the road triangle opposite Mistley Towers. Many Harwich smacks were built at Mistley for a Manningtree owner. In 1854 the Manningtree smack owner moved to Grimsby, and this ended Harwich's days as a major North Sea fishing centre.

In 1844 the Mistley Estate was sold in

Harwich sits on the point between the River Stour and Harwich Harbour.

The 1667 Navy Dockyard crane, at Harwich

The Pilot Station at Harwich

Harwich in 1934. The former Royal Navy Dockyard on the point. One of the last vessels built here was the sailing barge *Thalatta*, in 1910

individual lots and the Hall was pulled down. The nineteenth century saw a row of tall brick mills and maltings being built along the quay and a fleet of sailing barges brought imported foodstuffs from the London Docks. The waste from the mills was swept into the River Stour and this fed the second largest flock of swans in England. Mistley, as a mill port, was always rather a quiet place, although there was plenty of activity when barges were being unloaded.

The Horlocks all descended from Robert Horlock who moved here in 1832 and dominated Mistley in the sailing barges era. The Horlocks were all very competitive, as owners and racing skippers. The most successful owner was Fred Horlock who, in the inter-wars years, built up the largest shipping firm in Essex.

In 1900 Fred Horlock bought the new wooden sailing barge *Reliance*, The first barge he owned outright. Shortly afterwards he got a regular contract carrying acid in glass jars from London to the BX works at Brantham. Because

acid spillage would have damaged a wooden barge Fred bought the 85ft Dutch built steel sailing barge *St Eanswythe* that became a very successful earner. Fred was very progressive and in 1906 he ordered his first steam coaster, the *Mistley*. Over the next four decades Fred Horlock owned some twelve steamers, the largest of which was the 3,920 gross ton *Coralie Horlock* that traded in the China Sea. He also owned motor ships and was involved with over twenty steamers and motor ships in all, some of which he only owned for a short period. The F.W.Horlock's steam coasters appear to have been run quite separately to his barge fleet, which fed the Mistley mills and maltings.

In 1920 Fred built a shipbuilding yard on land below Mistley Quay. George Tovell had built barges here, which had ended with the barge *Colne Valley* in 1860. After building two steamers at the shipyard Fred built the steel sailing barge *Repertor* in 1924, which seems to have been very similar, and was an

The bawley *Bona* off Harwich, 2010. The bawley was the type of fishing boat used at Harwich, Southend and Leigh-on-Sea. Boilers were fitted to these, so that they could cook the shrimp on the way home, they became known as 'boiler boats' and this was corrupted into the term 'bawleys.' The *Bona* was one of the fine lined bawleys built by Aldous at Brightlingsea. The Harwich builders, Canns also built fast bawleys, while the Norman Brothers bawleys, such as the *Band of Hope*, were not so shapely

The spritsail barges *Adieu*, built of steel, at Mistley in 1929, and the *Gladys*, built of wood by Canns, at Harwich in 1896

The yacht moorings at Wrabness, 2008. The River Stour is very exposed but pressure for space led to it being developed for yacht moorings in the second half of the twentieth century

Skipper Jim Stone and his Mistley crew on the Mistley barge *Reminder* after winning the Thames and Medway barge race 'bowsprit class' in 1929. The Mistley skippers only raced with a crew from other Mistley barges

improvement on his successful *St Eanswythe*. By this time most owners were just starting to give up sailing barges, but Fred Horlock went on to build seven more.

Horlock's yard no. 10 was the 88ft steel sailing barge *Blue Mermaid* which was registered in May 1930 and named after one of Fred's race horses. Her sister barge was the *Resourceful*, yard no 11, registered in April 1931, making her the last full-sized sailing barge built for cargo carrying. The *Resourceful* was converted to a motor barge in 1933 but the *Blue Mermaid* went on under sail she was sunk by a mine in 1940.

After Fred's death in 1935 the company, run by his son Marcus, became M.F.Horlock & Co. Their last sailing barges were the steel *Portlight* and *Xylonite* which where sold in 1956. Horlock's *Resourceful* and *Reminder* became one hatch motor barges taking thousands of tons of ballast away from a dredger that worked up the River Stour. Horlocks sold off the last of their barges in about 1972, but the shipyard kept going as a base for tugs and craft used in dock repair, and Mistley staged a comeback as a port with larger coasters.

TW Logistics recently bought Mistley Quay and in the face of great local anger fenced it off. In 2008 there was a public protest and a large fleet of yachts sailed up to the quay to protest about the quay's closure. TW Logistics claimed they had fenced off the quay for 'Health and Safety reasons,' but in the autumn of 2009 a yacht got into difficulties near Mistley Quay and the rescue services had to cut a hole in the fence to save the four people on the yacht.

MANNINGTREE

Manningtree is effectively the highest point up the River Stour that sea-going boats of any size

The spritsail barge *Reminder* off Clacton. Built in 1929, the *Reminder* became a Maldon charter barge when her trading days finished.

can reach now, but sailing barges used to go to the Green Brothers mill at Brantham. Their barge, *Orion* was trading up here until 1938 loaded with ninety tons of wheat. Locals tell me the river was then pronounced 'Stouwer' on the Essex side and 'Stooer' on the Suffolk side. Manningtree was also a small port and the last sailing barge to bring a freight up here was the *Memory*, with timber, in about 1959, The *Ethel*

Ada was a houseboat here for a while in the 1960s, but since then yachts and moorings have taken over the river.

The first regatta at Manningtree appears to have taken place in 1845. Regattas in the Victorian period were mainly rowing races that were very keenly contested. Rowing dropped out of favour and after the Stour Sailing Club was established in 1936 sailing races became the main events. More recently there has been a series of tug-of-wars in the mud at low tide, and a race across the river.

In the old rowing regatta, only men rowed, and some races were seven miles down to Wrabness and back. In other races the boats had to have a passenger, dating back to the days when these boats were used for ferrying people. In 2009 the Manningtree Paddle and Oar Festival was started and in the new Festival there were classes for both men and women and mixed events.

Manningtree Regatta's most unique race is for sailing duck punts. In the nineteenth century gun punts were used in the winter on all East Coast estuaries to shoot wildfowl that were then sold for food. These punts were fitted with large muzzle-loaded shotguns, more like cannons than sporting weapons, and the duck punt was paddled quietly towards the flocks of wildfowl on the water. The wildfowler then hoped to shoot as many duck and geese as possible.

In the summer, at the local regattas, these punts were raced under sail. As duck punting went out of fashion most regattas dropped their punt races, but the Lucas family continue racing punts at Manningtree. At West Mersea a narrower racing punt has been developed, but the Manningtree punts have been kept close to their original design, although they are lighter than the old working fowling punts. At the 2009 Manningtree Regatta the five punts were all sailed by members of the Lucas family, aged between seventeen and seventy-eight.

STOUR NAVIGATION

It is believed that from earliest times goods were transported by boat up the fresh water River Stour. In 1713 a 24-mile long navigation was opened, linking the tidal Stour with the town of Sudbury. At its height in the mid-nineteenth century 65,000 tons a year were taken from the Mistley wharves up the Stour Navigation. One of the contractors employed to build the Stour

The eighteenth-century Swan Basin and Adam Pavilion behind Mistley Quay. In the background are the Mistley Workshops that were formerly a Granary.

Swans on a sandbank off Mistley Quay, 2008. This sandbank has built up since the 1950s.

Navigation came from the Fens and it is assumed that he introduced the Fen style barges. The horse-drawn 47ft 'Stour lighters' were operated in gangs of two, the cabin was on the aft 'house lighter', and each loaded 15tons. The use of lighters on the Stour finished in 1928 and in 1971 two barrages were constructed across the River Stour, ending navigation from the tidal river to the fresh water river.

The artist John Constable put Stour lighters into his landscapes and one of his paintings was of a barge being built in a dry dock at Flatford. When the Basin at Flatford was cleaned out in 1982 a lighter was found sitting on the blocks just where her skipper had left her when he died. The River Stour Trust was formed in 1968 as a pressure group to get the Stour Navigation re-opened. In 1973 the Trust dug out and repaired one of the lighters, a leading barge sunk in 1914, and renamed it *John Constable*. This Stour lighter has had a chequered career, but in 2010 the Heritage Lottery Fund gave £100,000 for her to be rebuilt at Pioneer Yard, Brightlingsea. As this

lighter was about hundred years old it may well have been in John Constable's paintings and the National Trust wanted it kept near the dry dock at Flatford for trips.

At Dedham, George 'Fred' Smeeth built small yachts and boats at the old coal wharf and hired out rowing skiffs until he died of a heart attack in 1979. His brother Albert ran the business for about another ten years when new owners took over and had new rowing skiffs built. Boat hiring continued, and in about 2002 part of the boat shed was turned into an attractive restaurant.

WALTON BACKWATERS

The Walton Backwaters are not an estuary with a fresh-water river flowing into it, but simply low-lying land that has flooded, leaving it dotted with marsh islands. The main channel is Hamford Water and the Backwaters are creeks branching off it on either side.

To many of my generation Walton Backwaters reminds us of Arthur Ransome's

A sunken reef of former Thames lighters, protecting Horsey Island. 2004.

wonderful fictional children's story 'Secret Waters.' In 1946, I was given a copy of 'Secret Waters' and read it in the dormitory at night after lights out. For a rather lonely boy of nine it opened up a wonderful world of adventure in the muddy waters of the East Coast. I am not sure that I have ever quite grown out of the thrill of 'Secret Waters,' but I am absolutely certain I don't want to.

Surprisingly Arthur Ransome's mysterious islands, surrounded by winding shallow creeks, and mysterious figures moving on the skyline, are still there. There is no real public vehicle access to Walton Backwaters and it is only possible to visit this group of marsh islands and creeks by boat or on foot. There are public footpaths around most of the Backwaters, but all the islands are privately owned and there is no landing without permission.

The Town Hard, at the very top of Walton Creek, is the only public landing for boats on the Backwaters, and this is only briefly accessible at high water. This is why the Backwaters retain

their 'Secret Water' feeling, and long may it last. Of course there are hundreds of yachts kept here at the Walton boatyards, at Titchmarsh Marina or on moorings in the Walton Channel and in the Twizzle Creek.

The 'Backwaters' are a series of creeks leading from Hamford Water up to Walton, Great Oakley Dock, Lower Kirby Quay, Landermere Quay, and Beaumont Quay. A Cut was dug by hand to get barges up to Beaumont Quay, at the head of the Backwaters. There were granaries on stilts at Landermere and Lower Kirby Quay where barges used to load grain and commercial ships still go up to the explosives factory at Great Oakley, an area closed to the public.

The shallow waters of the Backwater creeks attract a huge amount of wildlife, particularly in the winter. In the old days the Walton punt gunners used to leave Foundry Dock or Eagle Hard, at the entrance of Walton Creek, and spent all the tide rowing around the creeks looking for wildfowl to shoot. Sometimes they

Joe Backhouse at his sheep farm on Horsey Island, 2010.

The last of the Arab horses on Horsey Island.

got none, but one gunner is remembered returning with eighty-four duck. A committee of wildfowlers and conservationists run the management of the Backwaters. Although this group have opposing views on wildlife, they appear to work well together.

WALTON CHANNEL

Walton on the Naze is divided into two quite different places. There is a small resort on the seafront, while the Walton Channel cuts up behind the town. After entering Hamford Water yachts turn southeast into the Walton Channel, with low-lying marshes on both sides. On the eastern side of Walton Channel is a group of low islands, little more than sandbanks, called Stone Point. In the 1930s there was a holiday camp here with a Bar and beach huts, but the whole place burnt down. After this, the beach at Stone Point was abused with fires and general mess from parties and it became the

second place on the East Coast where fires were banned. Since 1996 the Walton and Frinton Yacht Club have worked hard to protect this nature reserve, particularly during the nesting season.

On the western shore of Walton Channel are Three Corner Island and Hedge End Island, with the slightly higher ground of Horsey Island in the distance. At some point there has been an attempt to reclaim Hedge End and it has a wall around it, but it floods with the tide. A rough ford was built to link it with Horsey so that wildfowlers could walk across, but the sheep from Horsey sometimes get trapped on the saltings, by the tide. In 1963 a wildfowling group bought the marsh islands of Hedge End and Three Corners, and have acquired further areas of saltings since then.

Walton creek leads off to the back of Walton town from the Twizzle. There was a windmill and a tide mill at the head of Walton Creek,

Sheep near the 'borrow ditch' behind the river wall at Ambrose Point, Horsey Island. This is the site of the *Swallows and Amazons* camp and the pond was created in an attempt to wall off The Wade. According to legend the wall across to Honeypot Island was completed, but broke on the first high tide.
Horsey is everything an Essex island should be. People live there, it produces food and it provides habitat for wild life.

Seals on Horsey Island, 2010. The seal colonies behind Horsey and in Oakley Creek have appeared since the 1950s.

where brigs and schooners used to take wheat from the rich farmland of the Tendring Hundred to the north of England and return with coal. Walton tide mill was pulled down in 1920 and the post mill blew down shortly afterwards. The Walton Sailing Club, started in 1912, had a clubhouse built on the point where the windmill had been, and this was later renamed Walton & Frinton Yacht Club. The boatyards then grew up as yachting increased in popularity. The Foundry Creek, near the entrance of Walton creek, was dammed off after the 1953 Floods and there is a low water landing here.

In the 1950s there were only the occasional seals visiting the Backwaters and few geese, but by about 1980 two seal colonies, mostly common seals with some grey seals, began to form. These are mostly near the explosive works in Great Oakley Creek and a smaller colony in Kirby Creek. Geese, marsh harriers and egrets have also returned to the Backwaters and are a common sight.

HORSEY ISLAND

The 300acre Horsey is the largest of the islands in the Backwaters and is Joe Backhouse's farm. Joe's family have been here since 1939 and he seems to enjoy the life on this quiet grassland farm. He says he chooses a breed of sheep that can swim well. They certainly need to, because at low tide the island is joined to the mainland by a mile-wide basin of grey mud. The causeway over the Wade links Horsey to Kirby (although it is part of the parish of Thorpe.) A vehicle can

drive across the causeway for about four hours out of every twelve-hour tide. A speedboat is kept at the jetty on Horsey to cross at high tide. The farmhouse is on the highest part of the island and was not flooded in 1953, but the two farm workers' cottages were flooded.

This used to be an arable farm a century ago and barges took crops away from a quay at the sheltered south-western end of Horsey. The quay has gone, although there is rickety landing jetty here, near a quarry dug in an attempt to build a wall to Honeypot Island. This is still a point of departure because Joe's half brother keeps a light aircraft on this end of Horsey.

In a north-east wind the Backwaters are very exposed and the marshes on the eastern side of Horsey are under real threat of erosion. The eastward end of Horsey has been saved, so far,

by an extremely imaginative scheme pushed through by Mark Johnson of the Environment Agency. Between 1984 and 1991 a series of steel London river lighters were sunk on the foreshore to act as breakwaters. Later, silt, dredged from Harwich Harbour, was pumped in behind the sunken lighters and on the saltings to heighten them. This was a brilliant form of protecting saltings and far cheaper than flooding land. It will save Horsey from simply vanishing into the sea. In the autumn of 1998 Harwich Haven Authority recharged Stone Point with some 200,000tonnes of dredged spoil. More, smaller re-charging was also carried out near Titchmarsh Marina.

Horsey is a very fragile island as it is low lying and takes the full force of the waves crashing in from the open sea. If Horsey was washed away

The ferro-cement barge yacht *Amadillo* in Kirby Creek, in front of Creek House.

Cottage above lower Kirby Sluice

the sea would eat out the whole area of the north-east corner of Essex.

SKIPPER'S ISLAND

Just to the west of Horsey is the 160-acre Skipper's Island owned by the Essex Naturalists Trust. On maps, the channel between Horsey and Skipper's Island is called Kirby Creek, but in the past it was called The Western Water. In this channel, just after World War II, William Backhouse started an oyster fishery and this was taken on by Frank Bloom, followed by his son Owen Bloom from Walton.

At the top of Kirby Creek is the tiny Honeypot Island, a patch of saltings that used to be shaped like a honeypot. From Honeypot, past a few local yacht moorings, the channel turns west and cuts in behind Skipper's Island. There are two rough causeways across this channel, one leading to the Warden's Hut on Skipper's Island.

KIRBY

The main Kirby Creek leads from the Wade up to Lower Kirby Quay. There used to be a horseshoe bend at the entrance of this creek, but a straight channel was dug for barge traffic and the old bend has completely silted up. At the end of the creek a shallow channel runs to the west to an area, at the bottom of Coalies Lane, known as The Old Quay, and remains of coal, brought in here, have been found. More recently it has been a peaceful spot where local people come to swim.

Since the bottom of Kirby Creek is hard ground, native oysters thrive and local, two-man boats, worked here in the 1600s. In the early twentieth century the little Maldon smacks used come up here in the summer and dredge young oysters when earnings were poor in the Blackwater.

Sailing barges used Lower Kirby Quay, at the head of the creek. The Granary here was

Arthur Ransome's yacht *Nancy Blackett* at the Walton & Frinton Yacht Club, 2009.

The newly restored 1900 Walton life boat *James Stevens No 14*, 2009. The people in front of the *James Stevens* are the descendants of the original RNLI lifeboat crew.

Lifeboats greeting the arrival of the new Walton & Frinton lifeboat *Irene Muriel Rees*, April, 2011. These are the Harwich lifeboat, the new Walton & Frinton lifeboat, Walton's existing lifeboat, the Walton inshore RIB, the *James Stevens No 14* and the Clacton inshore RIB.

converted to Quay House in 1936 and has since been raised one and a half metres to be above flood level.

Just above Lower Kirby Quay House is the Pilot's House. The last pilot here was Mr Scrogins and the practice was that when he saw a barge's tops'l coming up the Western Water he walked down the river wall on the eastern side of the creek to Peter's Point. Here, the pilot walked across the saltings, most of which have eroded away by crabs, to a jetty and rowed down to meet the barge.

In 2010 work was progressing to flood the marshes behind Peter's Point. Marshes were being flooded on Walton Backwaters because Britain had signed up to an International agreement to create bird habitat. Aerial photographs show that shore crabs, digging burrows, are destroying the Backwater saltings at a greater rate than a slight rise in sea level.

There was enormous local protest about the flooding of the Peter's Point marshes because it destroyed the habitat of kingfishers, owls and many other species found on grassland.

THE TENDRING COAST

WALTON ON THE NAZE

FRINTON ON SEA

HOLLAND ON SEA

CLACTON ON SEA

JAYWICK

LEE-OVER-SANDS

WALTON ON THE NAZE

Walton sits on a little piece of Essex sandwiched between the Backwaters and a wide Thames Estuary channel called the Wallet. Walton is not on the road to anywhere, except perhaps the Naze, the headland just to the north of the town. Walton, sitting alone on its peninsula, has the island mentality and people are fiercely loyal to it.

The sandy beaches from Walton down to Holland Haven gently slope out into the sea and break the force of the waves, but in really bad on-shore gales, waves surge up the beach and eat away at the cliffs. Erosion is a real problem to Walton and the Naze, every year a little more land slides into the sea.

In 1825 the first attempts were made to develop Walton as a seaside resort. The first wooden Pier was built in 1830 followed by the Marine Parade in 1835. The original resort consisted of lodging houses near the sea, but after World War II Walton took on a new direction and the resort's visitors mainly stayed in the caravan parks behind the town.

The first time I sailed past Walton in 1953 we witnessed a small lifeboat rescue. A maroon burst over the town and not long afterward the RNLI lifeboat left its mooring near the Pier and went round to a yacht anchored on the other side.

Our skipper, Arthur Hunt, was very dismissive of the whole brief affair, saying that the elderly couple on the yacht had just got 'in a funk.' He then became very angry, pointing at the Walton lifeboat and said 'there they go, longshore sharks, preying on the misfortunes of the poor sailormen!'

At the time I thought this outburst was more than a little unfair, after all, the lifeboat men had given up their time voluntarily to go

The Tower on Walton Naze was built in about 1720. Where the coast has been defended it has not eroded, but in places the poor defences have led to bad erosion on the Naze. Barge skippers were not above teasing people that the tower was actually a Roman well and the coast had eroded away!

A 70m groyne on Frinton beach, 2009. These breakwaters hold the beach in place and a long sloping beach uses up the force of the breaking waves before they hit the foot of the sandy cliff.

to the aid of seafarers in trouble. But Arthur, his brown weather-beaten face scowled at the lifeboat, remembering that salvaging ships had been a good earner for the longshore fishermen before World War I.

Walton was typical of the East Anglian landings and the Victorian 'private lifeboats' had basically been commercial ventures. Wealthy visitors to Walton often put up the capital to build the lifeboats, but the men who manned them saved lives first, and hoped that salvaging would reward them for their time. When the Royal National Lifeboat Institute opened a station at Walton, they were in competition with other lifeboats to start with.

In the Victorian period the RNLI favoured rowing self-righting lifeboats, but the East Anglian beach men would have nothing to do with these. For over a century they had been successfully salvaging ships with their sailing yawls and galleys so that south of Cromer, the RNLI used the North and

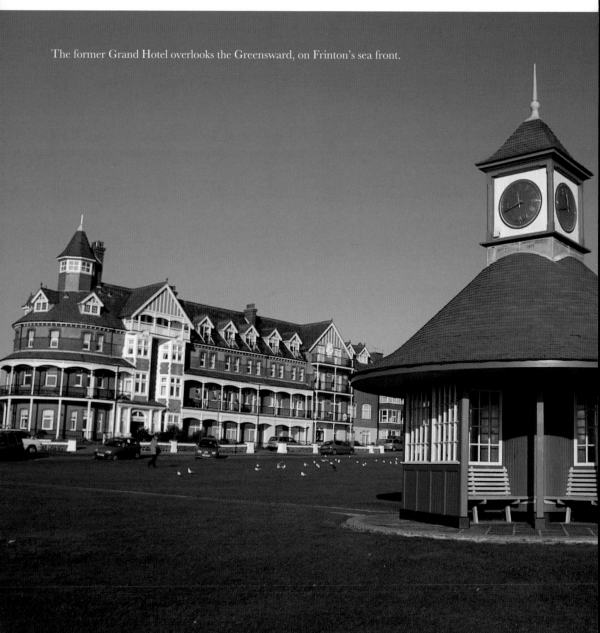

The former Grand Hotel overlooks the Greensward, on Frinton's sea front.

Suffolk sailing lifeboats. These were basically a more seaworthy version of the beach yawls that had been used for salvaging. They kept the dipping lug foresails because they could always be lowered quickly and they had large crews to dip the lug round the mast in heavy weather. The salvage smacks from the River Colne had gaff sails and had too deep a draft to go alongside vessels on the sands.

The second Walton RNLI lifeboat was the 43ft Norfolk and Suffolk *James Stevens No 14*

(James Stevens had left money for building twenty new lifeboats.) In 1905 the RNLI decided she would be one of the first lifeboats to be fitted with an engine, a 40hp Blake petrol engine. However she continued to use sails.

After a long career the *James Stevens No 14* became a houseboat. Then the Frinton & Walton Heritage Trust bought her and with a grant from the Heritage Lottery Fund and others they rebuilt her. She was re-launched in 2009 and became the oldest motor lifeboat in the world.

FRINTON-ON-SEA

Frinton had a population of about thirty in 1850, but by 2009 this had risen to about 6500, of which about half were retired. Frinton was created for people to live near the sea, not just to visit the seaside. This attitude has made it quite different from other resorts.

When you sail down the Wallet, the grass of Frinton's Greensward stands out, but the beach huts are all the same grey colour in contrast to the bright colours of Clacton and Walton on either side. Frinton is a little bit of Edwardian England that has lived on into the twenty-first century almost unchanged.

Although Frinton has pushed inland, the main town remains along the seafront and up to the railway line. Frinton is a good piece of Victorian town planning. The Esplanade, the seafront road, runs the length of the town and is set well back from the cliff edge. Between the Esplanade and the cliff is the wide-open Greensward, a name that suggests the Elizabethan England of Shakespeare. The people of Frinton love this open green space as it gives a great sense of tranquillity. They have the best of both worlds, a smart little commuter and retirement town with the feeling of a seaside village.

The people of Frinton have become renowned for their refusal to have the normal attractions of a seaside resort, arguing that with Walton and Clacton on either side there

Holland-on-Sea in about 1950. Here the groynes are holding the beach in place well. The Tendring coast from the Naze to the Colne, is well defended, as the whole coast should be.

was no need for them. Towards the end of the twentieth century a bitter local battle was fought to prevent a pub from being opened in the town, but in the end the first one, the 'Lock and Barrel,' was opened in a former shop in Connaught Avenue. The town has also accepted a fish and chip shop and even ice creams sold on the seafront in the summer. This was as far as Frinton was prepared to go. There are no cafes or shops on the Esplanade and, as a lady in one of the cafes in Connaught Avenue put it, 'that is the way it should be.'

The streets at the northern end of the seafront have the names Eton, Winchester, Oxford and Cambridge. Up-market English towns that don't give a hint that Frinton is actually in Essex. In Victorian times building materials for the new town were discharged from sailing barges on the open beach at Frinton but that is about its only connection with the sea. The Esplanade runs down past the very smart, well-kept houses, and the former Grand Hotel built in 1896, as far as the golf club on the edge of Holland Haven marshes.

The seafront public conveniences on the Esplanade seem to sum up Frinton's uniqueness. They are spotlessly clean, and a polite lady attendant still charges you to enter. Most small places have given up having attendants, but Frinton does not change easily and likes to keep up standards. The results justify the methods; Frinton 'through the railway's gates' remains a pleasant and friendly place,

The railway level crossing is the only way into the original town and its gates made it virtually a 'gated community.' when Network Rail mooted the idea of removing the wooden level crossing gates altogether there were howls of protest from the good people of Frinton. The Frinton Gate Preservation Society fought a three-year campaign to keep the gates that only ended when Network Rail had them removed during the night.

The railway crossing gave Frinton such a sense of being cut off from the rest of world that it seemed appropriate that the Frinton & Walton Heritage Trust have turned the gatekeeper's cottage and its garden into a little

Clacton in about 1910, with 'Trippers' promenading on the pier.

museum. It is perhaps ironic that in a town of up-market houses they have chosen to preserve one of the few workingman's houses in the place, but their enthusiasm for preserving the gatekeeper's cottage makes it worth a visit.

CLACTON-ON-SEA

As an adventure, as a teenager I used to go out to Clacton with a group of young people on a Saturday night. One of the places we went to was the 'Blue Lagoon', a dance hall on Clacton pier. It was bright and cheerful, but complete escapism. The decoration might have suggested a blue lagoon, but there was nothing tropical about the breezy seafront at Clacton. We didn't care; Clacton was a place you went to for enjoyment.

The resort of Clacton-on-Sea grew out from the area around the pier. It seems that the pier was started in 1869 and was developed further when it belonged to the General Steam Navigation Company. They had a fleet of paddle steamers that brought visitors from the Pool of London to the East Anglian resorts, calling at the piers. The General Steam Navigation Company did everything in their power to make the coastal resorts attractive to visitors. In recent decades the *Waverley*, the only remaining pleasure paddle steamer, has called at Clacton Pier and I noticed how hard she banged against the wooden pier head in a modest sea. In 2009 the owner of the Clacton pier, Billy Ball, decided to spend £3m on renovating the pier, including a new pub, as Clacton was catering for day trippers by then.

In the days when cargoes for Clacton arrived by sea, the barges were not allowed to use the pier, which was reserved for steamers. Instead there was a short pier at the end of Wash Lane. This pier had a steam crane where coal was discharged, and ice came here from Norway. However because of the high cost of using the pier, the barges often discharged on the open beach. Smeed Dean and Brice's barges brought in flint, brick rubble, bricks and cement for road-making. Generally the barges tried to discharge in one tide and horses on

Clacton Pier, 2009. The wind farm in the distance, on the Gunfleet Sands, opened in 2009.

Fairclough's cart used to wade into the water as soon as the tide was slightly down. It was not a good place to discharge. In February 1900 Smeed's *Victoria* was discharging brick rubble when she was caught by a southwesterly gale. The barge was almost blown up to the sea wall, where she would have been smashed to pieces, but the pier master got lines on her to prevent her from being wrecked and the barge was hauled off when the wind dropped.

Erosion is a problem all along the Tendring coast, but at least there has been a serious attempt to defend most of this coastline. The most dramatic parts of the sea defences are two stone breakwaters, at the southern end of Clacton. These breakwaters created Martello Bay, effectively a small harbour and two fishing boats are based here.

From the sea front at Clacton the wind farm on the Gunfleet Sands can be seen. Opened in 2009 the Gunfleet has 48 turbines with a

substation in the middle for relaying the power ashore. This was the sixth wind farm, at sea, to be opened in Britain.

JAYWICK

In Essex the word 'wick' is believed, to have meant 'sheep path.' St Osyth Priory once had 4000 sheep drowned by a surge tide on grazing marshes that are now believed to be out under the sea in front of Jaywick. This was recorded because the Abbey asked the King if they could be let off paying taxes.

The remaining marshes were grazed by sheep until 1928 when an enterprising estate agent divided the open marsh up into plots of about 16ft x 110ft and sold them off to people from the East End of London for about £5 a plot. On these plots small makeshift houses were built, often just huts made of crates or old railway carriages. The site was divided up into Austin Avenue, Rover Avenue, Daimler

Kite surfer and fishing boats at Martello Bay, Clacton, 2009. The stone placed on Clacton and Jaywick beach forms fish tail groynes and successfully traps the sand from going off shore, and prevents erosion.

Avenue and Bentley Avenue. This holiday shantytown brought happiness and freedom to hard working East Enders, but town planners loathed them.

In the 1953 Floods thirty-seven people were drowned in this retirement community. A terrible tragedy and around 700 people were made homeless. When I first visited Jaywick in 1995, the southern end, on the coast, looked like a Third World township, but I gather it was given a European grant. When I returned fifteen years later Jaywick had its own stone breakwaters that had successfully built up the sand on the coast, and the whole place looked a lot more prosperous.

LEE-OVER-SANDS

In the Victorian period the railways led to the building of the coastal resorts and in the motor age, in the inter-war period, before planning regulations came in, all sorts of 'get rich quick'

jerry built holiday-settlements sprang up on the Essex marshes. Lee-on-Sands was one of these.

Lee began in 1932 when a company bought the land beside Horse Wash Creek, just behind Colne Point, and no doubt inspired by Jaywick, just along St Osyth beach, started to develop a holiday resort. Because this isolated settlement was sited on low-lying land the bungalows were built on stilts. Lee-over-Sands was intended to be a rather up-market resort with its own golf club and even an airfield, but it failed. It seems to have survived as weekend retreats for those who like solitude and don't mind if they are cut off by the tide.

In the 1953 Floods only the Macgregor family were living at Lee. Mr Macgregor was the marsh man who looked after the animals that grazed on the marshes and in the winter he dug the ditches clear, by hand. During the flood the Macgregor's climbed into their boat and rowed across the marshes to Wick Farm.

Guy Taplin, the Wivenhoe wildlife sculptor, has one of the chalets, built on stilts to keep it above the high tide line. Guy has turned scavenging on the tide line into an art form by turning driftwood and metal into wader bird and sea bird sculptures. His work is in many well known collections.

The Essex Wildlife Trust took over about 400 acres on Colne Point for brent geese, sanderlings, curlews, redshanks and terns. In 1995 the warden said they were fighting a losing battle trying to keep little terns' nests safe. People walked their dogs on the saltings and they were destroying nests.

Between Lee-Over-Sands and the vast holiday resort of Point Clear are Guy Smith's farms of Lee Wick and Wigboro Wick that have recorded the lowest rainfall in the British Isles. The land here averages only 19inches of rain a year and once got down to 12inches, which is officially a desert. At this point the Sun newspaper hired a Native North American to come over and perform a rain dance. To show how seriously they took the problem the Sun ran the story next to their Page 3 Girl. The Native Chief told locals that for £5,000 he would go anywhere, but it always rains eventually.

The *Molly T* fishing off Jaywick. The old smackmen called this Egypt Point, because there was good fishing here, and the Bible said that Egypt was the land of milk and honey

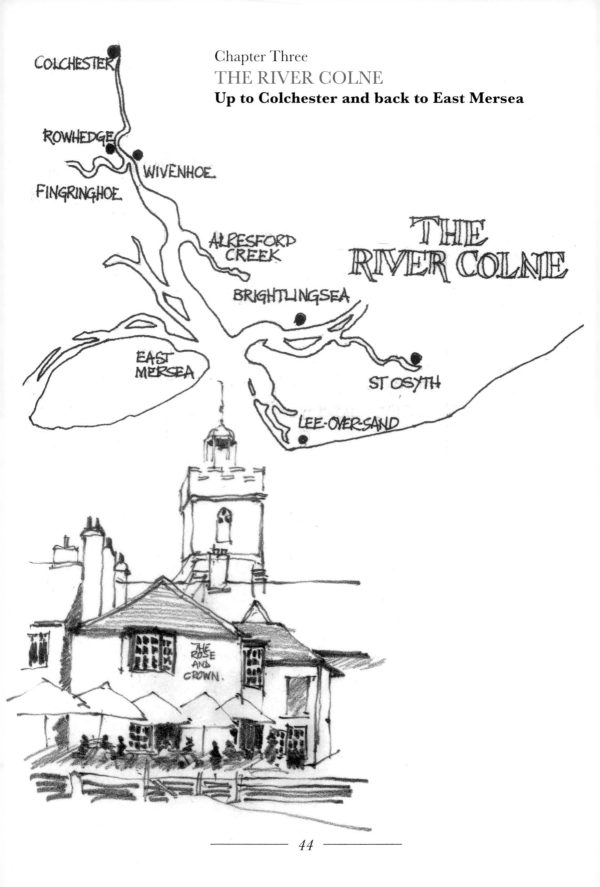

COLCHESTER

ROWHEDGE

WIVENHOE

FINGRINGHOE

ALRESFORD CREEK

BRIGHTLINGSEA

THE RIVER COLNE

EAST MERSEA

ST OSYTH

LEE-OVER-SAND

THE ROSE AND CROWN.

The 69ft Brightlingsea 'skillinger' smack *Pioneer* off Clacton. The *Pioneer* was built at Rowhedge in 1864, but by the 1940s was a houseboat at West Mersea. When the *Pioneer* was lifted out of the mud she still had the 'wet well' in which the live oysters were brought back to Brightlingsea. In 1998 the *Pioneer* was lifted out of the mud and totally rebuilt before sailing again in 2003. In her first season she revisited the Dutch Friesian island of Terchelling where the Victorian smacks used to dredge the big 'sauce' deep-water oysters. ˙

ST OSYTH

Pronounced 'Tosey' by the locals, the village's name originated from an Anglo-Saxon princess. St Osyth was the daughter of an Anglo-Saxon king and although she took a vow of virginity, her father made her marry King Sighere of the East Saxons, as a political alliance. Osyth was not a lady to be trifled with and according to legend she escaped and 'took the veil' to become a nun. Sighere, for his part, took the hint and gave the Lady Osyth an estate where she started a monastic order.

Unfortunately the site of Osyth's Priory was near the coast and raiding Danish Vikings set fire to it and captured Osyth and cut off her head. According to legend Osyth picked up her own head, ran off and then fell and died. Because of her brutal ending Osyth was made a saint.

In the Victorian period St Osyth creek was a busy barge port. There was a ' half tide' dock where barges lay alongside and horses with carts were at deck level, which made handling the cargo manually much easier. As well as the farm trade, there was a Maltings that was burnt down in 1920. The top of the creek had been dammed off to create a pond to trap the tidal water and power a tide mill. This mill, long derelict, blew down in about 1960. In the early 1930s, when lorries had taken much of the barge trade, there were twenty-two barges laid up at St Osyth, but a few barges came up here with freights after World War II.

In 1946 a boatyard was started in part of the old maltings. This yard was taken over by Andy Harman in 1987 and he successfully developed it with freelance shipwrights working on their own projects, mostly restoring wooden hulls.

Skipper James Green at the tiller of the smack *Pioneer* with father David Green freeing the mainsail and his daughter Bev Green on the stern. The *Pioneer* is a preserved part of Essex's maritime past, and fulfils a role in the modern world with charter work, mostly with young people.

Aboard the *Pioneer* on the Common Ground off Mersea Island with hand hauled dredges being thrown over the side, 2007. The deep-water dredges were larger and were hauled in with a capstan.

The best of these projects was the restoration and 'rigging out' the 80ft bowsprit barge *Edme* in 1992. The *Edme* was built by Cann at Harwich in 1898 and being a small barge used to trade up the River Stour to the old water mill at Brantham. She had taken acid in huge glass carboys and when spilt, it left circles on the hold ceiling (floor). She loaded about 110tons and became one of Brown's timber lighters at Heybridge in 1949 after she dropped out of trade.

By 2010 the once empty creek was packed with yachts laid up for the winter. According to local people so many people from 'Dagenham' (south Essex) have moved down into the village that it has changed its character. Certainly the old Essex speech has largely been replaced by Estuary English.

Between 1930-57 Samuel West's sailing barges used to come up to a jetty in the Ray Creek to load shingle that was brought down on a narrow gauge railway line. Barges also loaded on the open beach with a dragline crane and were then hauled off sideways, into deep water, by a single anchor. It was not realised at the time that shingle was a finite resource that could not be replaced and the coast needed it to stop erosion.

BRIGHTLINGSEA

The narrow streets in the older part of the town are always crowded with parked cars. If you are thinking of leaving your car parked on Brightlingsea waterfront, or for that matter across the creek at Point Clear, check the tide table. A Big Tide floods up to the Colne Yacht Club and up the road to French Marine Chandlery. Across the creek, water skiers who leave their vehicles carelessly parked on the foreshore can return to find the alarms going off as the tide floods the engines. Cars just don't like being in salt water.

The smack *G&A (George & Alice)* with a stownet being hauled, 2005. The channels are very narrow in the Thames Estuary and the fishermen had problems working drift nets so they continued the medieval practice of 'stall' netting, which was anchoring and lowering a huge bag net over the bow.

Sorting the catch, mostly herring, from the stownet on the smack *G&A*, 2005. 'Mac' Malcolm Macgregor is in the background. In the early 1950s he had crewed on some of the last Brightlingsea 'stowboaters.' Mac had made the net for Paul Winter, left, to experience this form of fishing after over fifty years.

The 30ft *Boadicea*, off Stone Point, East Mersea. This type of Colchester smack was just worked in the rivers and creeks.

Oystermen are dredging native oysters on a motorised smack, towing a skiff, on the 'Binnika' in the River Colne, 1950. Hervey Benham, when commenting on this period, said that the Essex fishermen were working smacks built for their grandfathers.

As the medieval Cinque Ports wanted to cash in on the North Sea fisheries, particularly the herring, Brightlingsea became an offshoot 'limb' of Sandwich. The Cinque is pronounced 'Sink' because that was the old French name given to the five ports in Sussex and Kent. This traditional link is kept alive each January by the Brightlingsea Freemen who choose a 'Deputy' for Sandwich. Each year in June the Mayor of Sandwich pays an official visit to the Mayor of Brightlingsea and there is a colourful procession through the streets.

The old smackmen used to call this mud haven 'Brit'lingsea Crik.' Here was a sheltered place where craft could easily get out into the Thames Estuary to go sea fishing. Its early origins were as a fishing port, but by the nineteenth century the Essex boats roamed all around the North Sea and English Channel in search of oysters as there were more smacks than

the local waters could support. In Cornwall the Essex smacks, with their CK registration, were looked on as being little short of pirates. They used to arrive in force, dredge up all the oysters and sail away again.

In 1864 the 'crab and winkle' railway line reached Brightlingsea and subsequently it became easy to land there and the town became a main centre of fishing in Essex. On any still evening in November the pleasant smell of sprats being processed pervaded the whole town. Fresh fish left the town in railway trucks, twenty-two trucks being the record in one day in the early 1930s, mostly destined for Belgium. When there was a surplus the sprat lay around in heaps waiting to be taken away for farm manure and the smell was absolutely appalling. In the Victorian period it was the same just up river at Wivenhoe and there are reports of eight thousand bushels of sprat being on the Quay in

Dan French, George Sweeny and Craig Morrison, crew of the Colchester Oyster Fisheries 'lucky' *Alexandra* at the Pyefleet jetty. They had just returned from dredging gygigas oysters on the 'Binnika', River Colne, 2010. Skipper Dan French said that 'Oysters are Essex.' He should know, because he is 'at least the sixth generation of Mersea oystermen'.

Jim Lawrence, barge skipper, sail maker and folk singer, sailing the *Native* in the Pyefleet with Pauline Lawrence and Janet Harker as crew, 2010.

heaps and the stench of rotting fish penetrating through the whole village.

Sprats that could not be sold, fresh, were smoked to preserve them. The smoke houses, just small wooden 'sentry boxes', were backyard operations. There were dozens of these smokehouses all over the town, and the oyster merchants Tabor, Musson, Day, White, Eagle and Minter were also involved in sprat sales.

In 1910 Mr Stewart of Newhaven in Scotland arrived at Brightlingsea and introduced pickling in barrels. This created a tremendous boom in sprat fishing because the market was considerably extended and fish were exported in barrels to Holland and the Baltic countries. Mussons, a Liverpool firm, had a yard in Tower Street, George Tabor Ltd, and also opened pickling yards. The Tabors were, in the 1930s, Billingsgate fish merchants, but like many other Essex fishing families they were descendants of sixteenth century Flemish Protestants who had fled religious persecution.

The Anglo-Swedish Preservation Union had the main pickling yard, started in 1914, on the waterfront, just behind the present 'smack dock'. Most of the yards used bay leaves for flavour, but the Anglo-Swedish had a secret recipe, which seems to have involved sandalwood that gave off a sweet smell. This yard appears to have closed during World War II.

James Edgar & Son of Deal established a cannery at Brightlingsea. They had the schooner *Gloria* anchored in the River Colne and fishermen unloaded directly into her. However in 1932 this firm went out of business and the machinery was sold to Lewis Worsp's North Sea Canners at Wivenhoe.

The dozen or so stowboaters left working after World War II used to go up to Wivenhoe to sell their sprat and the 'pair trawlers' did the same until the cannery closed in about 1960.

When Dick Harman joined the 43ft Brightlingsea smack *Charlotte Ellen* in 1951, it was virtually the end of the stowboating era. His father tried to discourage him from going in the smacks by saying 'the bloody things have drowned one half of our family and starved the other half'. Two of his mother's brothers had been lost stowboating, in the Swin, when the smack *Greyhound* was run down by a steamer, and other relatives had been lost in smacks in the Great Gale of 1881.

The oyster fishery in the lower Colne was a major local industry, but since oysters all looked the same there were considerable problems with poaching. Between 1891-1942 the Colne Fishery paid three quarters of the cost to the Colchester Borough Police Force that patrolled the oyster beds, day and night. The Colne River Police's sailing patrol boats were *Colne* (1895,) *Victoria* (1897) *Alexandra* (1901) and *Prince of Wales*(1904.) When this uniformed water police started, men were warned not to put their hands directly on the rail when going alongside a smack, as the smackmen would stamp on them.

With its narrow streets of terraced houses, old Brightlingsea is a typical nineteenth century industrial town. The industry was working the sea for oysters, fishing and shipbuilding. Over-fishing reduced fish stocks and there was no demand for the type of small commercial vessels that the two Brightlingsea shipyards built, so the town had to find other forms of economy. Some light industry appeared near the waterfront and the building of the Gunfleet wind farm briefly brought back some of the maritime glory of the old days, another form of harvesting the seas.

ALRESFORD CREEK

Alresford Creek is only navigable for about two hours either side of high water, but it has become the home to about fifty pleasure craft. This was one of the last places where there were no restrictions on swinging moorings and people could put them down free of charge. However three organizations claimed the creek bed and sought to charge them. The Alresford Creek Boat Owners Association first thought of fighting to keep the creek's moorings free but then chose to pay the Town of Colchester as

The 'spritty' barges of the Thames Estuary were built in many sizes. Here, anchored off Brightlingsea Creek, is the 41ft *Cygnet*, that was built for working up to farm wharves in creeks, and the 84ft *Marjorie* built for coastal work.

being the legal owners of the creek bed.

Just inside the mouth, lost in the mud, is the hulk of the smack *Xantha*, a noted fast sailer, built from the winnings of yacht racing. In the 1890s Bill Cranfield used to skipper the 60ft yacht *Xantha* during summer months, but returned home to Rowhedge to fit out his smack *Xantha*, for the winter stowboating, for sprat. The smack was laid up at the start of World War II and gradually fell to pieces. In the 1960s her lead ballast went into the smack *ADC* when she was rigged out to sail again.

A little further up Alresford Creek are the remains of the ballast-loading jetty. In about 1932 barges started to load ballast at this jetty, but the pit went over to road transport in 1958 and barge traffic petered out after this.

Some of the river walls surrounding the creek were built in about 1730. There were two crossings over Alresford Creek. At the mouth was a railway line, 'the crab and winkle,' to Brightlingsea. This was opened in 1866 and closed a century later. The ford, halfway up the creek, originally carried the Toll Road to

Brightlingsea. A man was employed to sweep the silt off the ford and in World War II the army used to drive over the ford. In the 1960s it was still possible to walk across the ford and boat owners kept the Alresford side clear so that they could use it as a landing hard, but the other side silted up with about 3ft of mud. In 2008 the local 4x4 club used a Landrover with a snowplough on the front to batter open the crossing.

Up until 1914 'stackie' barges loaded on the ford and at five other places in the creek.

The dock, at the head of the creek, at the Thorrington Tide Mill, could hold two barges and flour, haystacks and bricks were loaded here. Until about 1900 the barge *Lucretia*, owned by C. F. Frost of St Osyth, used to come into the barge dock about three times a year to load 30,000 bricks from the Husk & Harper brickfield.

The Tide Mill was built on elm trunks in 1831 and worked until 1926. Tom Glover purchased the derelict Mill and used it as a store for his seed business, and as he was very

The two main types of nineteenth century Essex fishing boats on Brightlingsea Hard, 2009. On the left is the beamy transom sterned 'bawley' *Helen & Violet* and on the right, the counter sterned smack, *Maria*.

keen on mills started to restore it. In 1974, T. A. Glover sold the Mill to Essex County Council who had the resources to finish the restoration.

WIVENHOE

The first time I took my wife Pearl out, we went to Wivenhoe, to look at the 112ft wooden barquentine *Cap Pilar*, that had been built in St Malo in 1911. We walked along the muddy foreshore, from the Anchor Hill to the abandoned *Cap Pilar*, a former Grand Bank cod fishery vessel. This barquentine had achieved fame from an adventure voyage, made around the world, in the late 1930s. She had been brought to Essex as a cheap place to be laid up and had just deteriorated there. I found this barquentine madly attractive and romantic, but I remember Pearl being very silent as we stood there in the rain. It was hardly an exciting day out for her. We never saw the *Cap Pilar* again.

We returned to Wivenhoe in the autumn of 1960, this time by water in *Sea Fever*, and berthed near the 'Rose & Crown.' The locals seemed pleased to see us, as Wivenhoe didn't get many visiting yachts, because there were very limited berths on the waterfront. The quay front where we lay that peaceful night has now greatly silted up and become saltings is some places. The smack *Victory* sits in a berth that needs a high tide for her to escape a few feet back into the deep main channel, while the smack *William* is on a mooring amongst the yachts. The *William*, built by Howard at Maldon in 1888, was built to dredge oysters in the narrow channels and had been owned by a cheerful syndicate of five local men.

Sitting in a sheltered valley, Wivenhoe seems far removed from the harsh realities of the open sea, yet it grew up as a fishing and shipbuilding centre. The fishing came first, because this is about as far up the River Colne that the smacks could reach easily. After this the river is very narrow and it was difficult for sailing craft to

The Smack Dock at Brightlingsea is just reserved for local smacks and former fishing vessels. On the left is the *William & Emily (Odd Times)* built in 1886, the *Nellie* 1888 and the *Iris Mary* 1911.

reach Colchester.

When Daniel Defoe visited Wivenhoe in 1724 he recorded that this was the main place for Colchester Native oysters. These he said were taken at the mouth of the 'Colchester Water,' presumably he was talking about the Colchester Oyster Fishery in the Pyefleet. Oysters were taken and stored on the Wivenhoe foreshore, but the river seems to have silted up and all trace of the storage pits gone.

The narrow River Colne was the birthplace of the Colchester smack, a type of Victorian fishing boat famed for its speed and manoeuvrability. To get up river to Wivenhoe, or indeed any of the Essex creeks, smacks had to be very handy and fast. A fast sailing hull had been developed for smuggling and the fishermen took their lines and used them for their smacks. In the Victorian period the Colne became a yacht building area and the Essex smackmen, many of whom spent the summer as professional crews on the great racing yachts, developed a passion for fast sailing. The smuggler's luggers and great racing yachts influenced the design of the fast sailing smacks of Essex. But it was rather a chicken and egg situation because the smacks and yachts were built alongside each other and ideas passed to and fro.

In the Victorian period the London businessman Charles Nottage based a large yacht at Wivenhoe. During the summer he employed fishermen as crew and to give them a better chance in life he set up the Nottage Institute in 1894 to teach navigation in evening classes. In 1947 'The Nottage' moved to its present premises on the quayside and wooden boat building was taught in evening classes. On the Nottage walls hang faded brown and white photographs, and ship portraits of the yachts and vessels, that were the pride of Wivenhoe in the proud days of the Empire. The Nottage Institute has partly turned into a unique local maritime museum.

The old town was split into the 'Up Streeters'

who lived up on the high ground, and often had a piano in the front room, and the 'Down Streeters,' who were the manual workers who lived down near the river and went to the pub for relaxation. In recent decades the area near the river has been the most sought after by people moving in. The pubs around the waterfront did well when Wivenhoe's fleet of smacks were sailing out into the Thames Estuary. It was said that Wivenhoe was a drinking village that had a fishing problem.

The picturesque houses along the waterfront catch the sun and used to flood, before the Colne Barrage was built. Most of the houses still have the low walls to keep high tides out, and at Maple Cottage they used to row to the pub. Once, on a big tide, the water flooded into the bar of the 'Rose & Crown,' but in good East Coast fashion the men stayed on drinking. Unfortunately George Cook had had rather too much to drink and started to argue with the landlord, who told him to get out. As George splashed his way towards the door he turned and shouted angrily 'I have swum out of better pubs than this one!'

Trade on the Colne mainly passed Wivenhoe by. Once on a fine summer's evening in about 1947 the people on the quay spotted a barge coming up river under full sail. Usually the spritsail barges had their bowsprits pulled up in the rivers, but the *Will Everard*, one of largest spritsail barges ever built, came ghosting up river with every sail set, trying to 'save her tide' with 280 tons of coal for Colchester gas works. In the hard winter of 1964 the army had to blast the ice out of the river so that the *Will Everard* could get up to the Gas Works with coal, from Keadby.

The Wivenhoe shipyards had a great reputation for building grand yachts and small commercial craft, but in the interwar years they were closed in a Government 'rationalization.' When World War II started there was suddenly a great demand for small ships and the new Wivenhoe Shipyard Co. started in 1939, to help with the war effort. As well as building ships, parts of the Mulberry Harbour for the D-Day landing on Normandy were built, just up stream of the old village.

Wivenhoe is not a suburb of Colchester, but an independent community with its own institutions. Wivenhoe has its own station, with some trains running directly to Liverpool Street in an hour and ten minutes, so that it is has become a commuter's town. The streets near the station are known locally as The Shipyard, for the obvious reason that there was shipbuilding here from at least the eighteenth century right up until Wivenhoe Shipyard Ltd closed in 1962.

Even in the 1960s, when the shipyards were still open, Wivenhoe had a colony of artists living in the streets beside the quay. When the concrete towers of the University of Essex were built some staff moved into Wivenhoe. Certainly the University has kept Wivenhoe's small bookshop open, when many similar shops in small towns have been forced out of business by the large national stores in the major towns.

The Ferry from Wivenhoe across to Fingringhoe and up to Rowhedge, that is run in the summer, is one of the successful community activities in the village. There was originally a ford at Wivenhoe, but in 1856 Colchester wanted large ships to go up river so they were given permission to dredge if they agreed to operate a rowing ferry at Wivenhoe 'for ever.' However horses and carts continued to use the ford at low tide until 1937, while the Fingringhoe men, who worked in the shipyards, crossed by ferry.

In 1956 Colchester wanted to close the ferry, but local people, led by Councillor Dorothy Cook and shipwright Derrick Allen, hired a bus and went to the High Court in London to fight their case. However the Lord Chief Justice ruled that Colchester had the right to close the Ferry.

When ships grew too large for Colchester, Wivenhoe and Rowhedge had a period as commercial ports. The timber wharf at Wivenhoe was constructed in 1969 and the last

In the age of sailing ships and basic navigation, wrecks were very common off the Essex coast. Brightlingsea had this warehouse, where wreckage was landed and stored before being sold.

Dave Wells working on the rebuilding of the East Coast Sail Trust's 88ft barge *Thalatta* at St Osyth, 2010. The East Coast Sail Trust originated from the Sailing Barge Preservation Trust that bought the Cann-built barge *Memory* in 1956. The idea was to keep her trading under sail after all the other barges had finished. After a bad cargo carrying survey, in 1960, the *Memory* became a charter barge, working from Mill Beach, Heybridge and because there was little money, the passengers slept in hammocks, in the open hold. In 1967 the mast and sailing gear were taken out of the *Memory* and transferred to the *Thalatta*, so that she could continue the sail training trips, with young people sleeping in hammocks.

freight here was in 1990. James Husk started shipbuilding, at the lower end of Wivenhoe waterfront, in the 1840s and James W. Cook, who owned 1,500 lighters on the Thames and needed somewhere to build and repair them, bought the yard in 1947. Cooks could build a lighter in three weeks because all the hull plates were the same size. Like all the Colneside yards, Cooks specialized in small commercial vessels and they found it increasingly difficult to get orders. I remember peering into the shipyard and seeing the hull of the *Lord Nelson* taking shape. The steel sail training barque *Lord Nelson* was a financial disaster and the hopper dredger *Kilmourne*, completed at Cook's in 1986, was the last ship built at Wivenhoe. The end of shipbuilding was a sad day because it had been the lifeblood of the Colneside villages.

COLCHESTER

The Iron Age and Roman port of Colchester was probably further up the River Colne, above the town. However the medieval port was the Hythe, which is the old word for a quay, and was some distance from the town centre. The best known boat builder associated with Colchester was Philip John Sainty who at various times was ship's master, ship owner, boat builder and smuggler. He was particularly good at building fast craft for smuggling and this led to the Marquis of Anglesey commissioning him, after he had got him out of jail, to built the yacht *Pearl* in 1820.

Sainty had been involved in smuggling goods such as brandy, gin, tea and tobacco and that had landed him in jail, but one of the earlier smuggled goods had been Tyndale's Bible, and

Prior's *Brenda Prior* leaving the cold grey waters of the River Colne with yet another cargo of ballast for the London construction industry, 2007. The Prior's Rowhedge ballast barges were the only coastal cargo vessels operating from the Essex Rivers, the sole successors of the once mighty fleet of sailing barges.

that was far more dangerous. It is believed that the first Bible in English was brought up the River Colne in boats rowed with muffled oars.

The Established Church's Bible was in Latin, which meant that only the clergy could read it and this had given them a monopoly of the Church services. William Tyndale (1494-1536) was a Protestant Reformer and he had translated the Bible into English and had it printed. The Bible was printed in Europe and smuggled over to England, but Tyndale was put to death in Belgium for making the translation. However, the Tyndale Bible eventually became the basis of the King James I Bible.

In the nineteenth century The Hythe was the centre of barge trade on the Colne. A regular trade was imported wheat from London Docks being taken under the Hythe Bridge up

to Marriage's East Mill. To reach the East Mills the barges lowered their 'gear'(masts and sails) and went under the Hythe Bridge at an hour and a half before High Water. Their rudders touched the bottom most of the way up and if the tide turned before they reached the mill they grounded on a shingle bank near the East Mill Bridge. The huffler, the pilot helping the crew, then climbed up a ladder to return home and came back to finish the trip on the next tide.

Marriage's owned several barges, including *Violet* and *Fleur-de-Lys*, but their best known barge was the *Leofleda*, named after the Saxon lady who had once owned the original mill. The *Leofleda* had been built in 1914 at the famous Harwich yard of J. & H. Cann. The barge was so well built that she was still carrying

Passing the Fingringhoe ballast quay, on the smack *Maria*, 2010.

View of the River Colne, past the Colne Barrier, to Prior's ballast quay at Rowhedge, 2009. A larger barge *Poller Rose* joined Prior's ballast barges *Nigel Prior* and *Bert Prior* to cater for the building of the Olympic village.

cargoes of flour nearly forty years later, with her original decks that had not made the cargo wet. The barge was sold to become a yacht and was reported to have sunk in the Gulf of Mexico later.

In 1921, when motor lorries started killing off the stackie trade, Josh Francis started buying up barges that had been in the farm trade. In 1933 he formed Francis and Gilders, (Gilders was a London broker who found the freights) and they operated fourteen sailing barges, mostly bringing grain and timber to Colchester. After World War II Francis and Gilders started to sell off their sailing barges and in 1954 they merged with the London & Rochester Trading Co, a Kent firm, that later became Crescent Shipping.

Headley Farrington, manager of the Colchester office, told me that Francis and Gilders kept several smaller barges, after Marriage's had sold the *Leofleda*, just to do the work up through the bridges to the East Mills. The Maldon stackie barge *Dawn* was ideal for this trade because she was a very low flat barge, but the *Millie* had to have her bitt heads sawn off so that she would fit under the bridges. The *British Empire* was a slightly larger barge which had to have her boat filled with water on the foredeck, to get her bow down, to go under the bridges. In 1954 she got stuck under the Hythe Bridge and the fire brigade had to pump her full of water to prevent the Hythe Bridge from being lifted up on the tide.

Gordon Hardy, when he became skipper of the *George Smeed*, looked forward to doing a cargo up to East Mills. When he got 'fixed' to go up there he found it very hard work, even with the help of a 'huffier'. The barge's 'gear' (mast and sails) had to be lowered on to the deck and hoisted up again four times, on the hand windlass. Being very relieved when he finally got back under the Hythe Bridge again, he was not happy when the office told him to do three more freights up there.

The East Mill trade ended in June 1955 when the *Kitty*, *Centaur*, *George Smeed* and *Mirosa*

were sold off. The *Mirosa* is credited with being the last barge to take a freight up to the East Mills, and she was one of the barges to be sold to Browns to become an unrigged timber lighter on the Blackwater.

Although the barge trade ended, because they were too small, Colchester became a boom port in the 1970-80s with vessels of 50-60m long and 1000tons discharging at the Haven and King Edward Quays. Often there were two or three ships waiting, anchored off Brightlingsea, for an empty berth at the up river wharves. In the narrow river the incoming ship went on to the outside berth and the vessel that had already discharged slid out and waited its turn in the swinging berth (which by 2009 had silted up.) The economics of shipping was demanding larger vessels and these just could not get up to Colchester. New wharves were built at Wivenhoe, Rowhedge and then Brightlingsea to take larger ships.

The suction of the mud at Hythe Quay sometimes prevented vessels from rising on the tide. The *Ivana* was discharging 5,500tons of coal at the Hythe in 1984 when the suction of the mud held her down as the tide rose. The firemen had to come with pumps to keep her afloat as water poured over her decks and into the hatches. She remained stuck for two days before breaking free.

Colchester waterfront became a sad place after the new road bridge was built across the river, in 1994,which cut off The Hythe. We sailed up in *Three Sisters* just before the bridge was built and the Hythe Quay area was already very run down and about ten years later we sailed up in *Mary Amelia,* avoiding the shopping trolleys that had been pushed over the quay. Colchester began the difficult task of regenerating its waterfront in about 2000.

ROWHEDGE

Rowhedge is a waterside residential centre on the west shore of the River Colne, eyeing Wivenhoe just across the river. The first time I

Looking up to Rowhedge from Wivenhoe, 2009. Wivenhoe waterfront was once the centre of fishing on the River Colne. The quays have silted up, possibly because craft are berthed here permanently.

The 'Rose and Crown' on Wivenhoe waterfront.

saw Rowhedge was in July 1968, when I came on a club outing to look at the new wooden 37ft gaff yacht *Odd Times*. We walked up the river wall from Wivenhoe and then crossed over on the Rowhedge Ferry and walked to Ian Brown's yard, on the lower end of the quay. Our guide was John Leather, who had grown up in Rowhedge, and had designed the smart new hull that was towering above us on the slipway. The mast was already stepped, ready for the launch in two days' time.

The Rowhedge era as a shipbuilding centre had already passed and it appeared to be a pleasant and quiet village. The previous year Browns had built the handsome 37ft gaff ketch *Celandine*. We wondered if this was the beginning of a new era of wooden boatbuilding, but it didn't last. No one foresaw that just over thirty years later both shores of the Colne would be lined with brightly coloured housing developments.

Although Rowhedge shares its history of fishing and shipbuilding with Wivenhoe, the two villages were deadly rivals in the past. Rowhedge is much smaller and has a very pleasant waterfront. There are two open riverside greens, Pearson Quay and Lion Quay. The Ferry Hard, and 'Anchor' pub, are in the middle of these two greens. Below Pearson Quay was the original 'Down Street' shipyard of Rowhedge. In the early nineteenth century Phillip Mossley Sanity built schooners and a 200ton barque here. Harris was next in this yard, building yachts and smacks, of which the smacks *Pioneer* and *Maria* are still sailing after being rebuilt. This yard became the Lower Yard of Rowhedge Ironworks Co. shipyard. When the Rowhedge Ironworks closed Ian Brown, who had moved up here from the Thames, continued yacht building and repairing until 1994.

By the time Rowhedge Ironworks closed in 1963 they had built 947 vessels, the largest of which was the 200ft tanker *Mahtab*. Amongst the many working ships built here was the *VIC 77*, a steam-powered Victualling Craft, built in 1944, to serve in the Naval Dockyards and Robert Simon of Rowhedge restored it in the 1970s.

When Ian Brown's yard closed there was

The barquentine *Cap Pilar*, at Wivenhoe shipyard, in about 1958.

Looking up the River Colne from Wivenhoe with the empty Rowhedge Wharf on the left.

an attempt to save one of the old sheds for a museum, but it was pulled down when the houses were built. In 2000 the Rowhedge Heritage Trust obtained a container and clad it to look like one of the old barge-boarded shipyard sheds with a tin roof, and this stands on the Lion Quay green,

At weekends in the summer, Rowhedge and Wivenhoe are linked by a popular ferry, which has become increasingly busy since the landing pontoon was placed on the Rowhedge side in 2009. In the past there was a ford between Rowhedge and Wivenhoe marsh and a ferry,

a punt, which ran when there was water in the river.

Down river, below Rowhedge Quay, is the Rowhedge Wharf, a monument to the boom years of shipping on the Colne. From the 1930s the port of Colchester, which later included Rowhedge and Wivenhoe, seems to have concentrated on bulk 'dirty' cargoes. In World War II Rowhedge Wharf was a wooden quay where sailing barges loaded ballast for building airfields and this wharf was enlarged and a warehouse built.

One of the Colne's peak periods was

during the Miner's Strike in 1984 when all twenty berths on the river were full and another eighteen ships were lying at anchor off Brightlingsea waiting for a berth, mostly loaded with coal from Poland and Germany.

Until 1989 the port was earning money for its owners, the Colchester Borough Council. The problem was that ships were getting larger, but the River Colne stayed the same size. It seems that the largest ship coming to Rowhedge was the 286ft (88m) *Sea Weser* in 1990. The Wivenhoe wharf closed that year and the last ship to discharge in the port of Colchester was

the 1,054gross tonne *Beveland*, at Rowhedge, in 1999. The wharf and port then closed and Colchester Borough Council obtained an Act of Parliament to close the port above the Barrier.

FINGRINGHOE

Although the rural Colneside village of Fingringhoe is cut off from the river, it is the last Essex port to have barge traffic working from the Ballast Quay. The Rowhedge Creek leading from the Colne up to Fingringhoe water mill was known as the Roman River. The wooden tide mill at the head of the creek was built in 1531 and was added to over the centuries. The brick built part of the mill was built as a steamroller mill in 1893 and, like many country mills, Fingringhoe produced animal food when the industrial roller mills in the ports had taken over the flour trade.

After World War II there was regular barge traffic up to the mill, even though the channel was shallow and twisting and regarded as being one of the most difficult places to navigate on the East Coast. Guy Harding, the Wivenhoe boatyard owner, acted as a huffler, guiding barges up the creek. Barges used to go into the creek on the early flood tide and kept moving slowly up the creek to reach the mill at high water.

Even then the deeply loaded barges sometimes got stuck. Once Crescent Shipping's *Northdown* went in the creek too deeply loaded. (The skipper and mate were paid on a share of the freight money.) Unfortunately the barge got stuck and couldn't reach the mill by high water. This trapped Sully's barge *Beatrice Maud* up at the mill for two weeks. The skipper of the *Northdown* claimed the tide 'had taken off' (been a small tide) but Crescent Shipping had to pay for *Beatrice Maud's* loss of earnings for that time.

The last operators of the mill were Hitchcock's Animal Feeds and I remember coming here in the early 1960s to collect a 14ton lorry load of 'bran.' This came down a chute in bags and I had to stop the bags with my hand

Fingringhoe Mill is at the top of the 'Roman River.'

and then carry them, on my back, to stack the Foden lorry. It was hot work, as the bags kept coming down at speed from somewhere above, and I was very relieved when I could shout that my lorry was full.

In the hard winter of 1963 the creek was closed with ice and lorries brought grain in by road from the Hythe. Barge traffic resumed and the barge skipper Bob Child, after he retired, went as mate on the last barge taking a cargo to Fingringhoe mill. This was in 1982, when a ship brought maize to Rowhedge Quay and Crescent Shipping's motor barge *Roan* took 220tonnes of maize up. The mill closed in 1993 and was converted to houses in 1997.

Opposite lower Wivenhoe, in front of the World War II pillbox, is the ruin of 'The Drop', built in 1708 to supply ballast for sailing ships in the coal and timber trade. In 1933 The Thames Sand Dredging Co had started a Rowhedge quarry to supply sand and stone for the London building trade. The quarry is still operating at Prior's Quay where their ballast barges load and make several runs a week to the London wharves. The Prior's business was started in 1870 and they originally had three of their own sailing barges carrying ballast to their wharves on the Thames. However these wharves were compulsorily purchased in the Dockland Developments. The Prior's barges are the last ones on the Essex coast carrying freights to the Thames wharves.

The War Office purchased much of the land around Geedom Creek, on the lower Colne in 1905, for 'manoeuvring purposes.' This wild area of saltings has remained an army firing range and they fly a red flag when live ammunition is being used.

EAST MERSEA

East Mersea is the peaceful end of Mersea Island. The pub is on the main road and near the Church overlooking the sea is a vineyard.

The Rev Baring-Gould became the vicar of East Mersea, in 1871, and later wrote his rather heavy Victorian novel 'Mehalah.' He certainly understood the brooding Essex marshes, but this bookish vicar did not get on well with local country people. They had nothing in common.

In 1999 the normally peaceful East Mersea was slightly ruffled when Leisure Great Britain decided to replace the beach huts on the sea front below Old Hall Farm with mobile homes. In the 1930s the East Mersea Golf Company had built seventy-two 12ft x 20ft beach huts for families to stay in. The idea was that the men played golf while their families played on the Sunny Beach on the East Hall Estate. Water was taken down from a well at the top of Church Lane and a pony and trap delivered the milk daily. During World War II the army took over the chalets and put up mock wooden guns to 'defend the position.' After the war the number of beach huts increased to 200 and the area became known as Cooper's after Owen Cooper Estates. In 1989 Cooper died and the estate was sold to a leisure group who knocked down sixty huts and started to redevelop the site for mobile homes. The Cooper's Beach Chalet Society, organized by Carol Rothon, fought a brave battle to try and prevent this happening.

At the far end of the Island the road peters out and there is a track down to the headquarters of the Colchester oyster fishery. This building is beside The Pyefleet, which is basically a large creek running behind Mersea Island. The River Colne and its creeks had been purchased by the Aldermen of Colchester from King Richard the Lionheart, in 1189, who had needed cash to repair Dover Castle. Since then the Borough of Colchester has owned this rich oyster fishery, but rented it out. In the Victorian heyday of the oyster fishery the income kept down the rates in Colchester.

The fishery was run from Brightlingsea and

The silted up Hythe Quay at Colchester, 2009. The Hythe, the Saxon word for quay, was the centre of trade to Colchester. Eventually trade moved down river to the Haven and King Edward Quay.

The smack *Our Boys* laying at Rowhedge and the new ferry jetty. 2009.

in 1908 there were some eighty-six smacks and the steam dredger *Pyefleet* engaged in the Colne oyster fishery. At the time oysters, after farming, was the largest industry in coastal Essex.

The Colchester oyster fishery had storage sheds on Brightlingsea waterfront and across the Colne, on Pewit Island, was the company shed with more storage pits. The first Packing Shed on Pewit Island was built in about 1888 and knocked down by the 1953 Floods but was replaced with a Nissen hut two years later. A series of hard winters in 1940, 1947 and again in 1963 destroyed most of the Native oysters in the Colchester fattening grounds in the Pyefleet and this caused the Colne Fishery Board to abandon the lease.

Christopher Kerrison, who continued to use Pewit Island as the base for a time, took up the lease in 1965 as a private venture. However, the cost of moving oysters and men across the river two miles to Brightlingsea led to the purchase of North Farm on the eastern end of Mersea Island. In 1981 a French-style store was built at North Farm and this became the fisheries packing and sales centre. When an oyster disease hit the fishery, Christopher Kerrison developed an international business, retailing oysters, lobsters and crabs and employed about twenty people. When the diseased subsided the cultivation of Pacific gygigas oysters was started, and in 2005 native oysters were cultivated again. The gygigas oysters can be harvested all the year round and thrive in shallow water, while the flat Native European oysters, which can only be harvested when there is an R in the month, prefer deeper water. The gygigas breed happily in the River Colne, but 'fatten' quicker in the shallow creeks.

At the top of Mayday's Marsh, in the Pyefleet, 'withies', branches cut from bushes, mark the oyster beds. The oysters are also fattened in Geeton Creek and across the River Colne on the Binnaka, off Brightlingsea.

Chapter Four
THE MIGHTY BLACKWATER
West Mersea around to Bradwell

THE STROOD

RAY CHANNEL

WEST MERSEA

SALCOTT CHANNEL

OLD HALL CREEK

TOLLESBURY

GOLDHANGER

HEYBRIDGE BASIN

BRADWELL

MALDON

OSEA ISLAND

NORTHEY ISLAND

THE MIGHTY BLACKWATER

MAYLANDSEA

THE STROOD

The Strood is the causeway connecting Mersea Island to the Essex mainland. Because a Roman villa was known to lie under West Mersea church it was assumed that the Romans had built the causeway. There is even a local legend that the ghost of a Roman soldier marches across the Strood, however he would have got very wet if he had tried this because the probable site of the Roman ford is about half a mile down the Pyefleet.

In 1978 contractors laying a water main to Mersea discovered that the causeway was on oak trees. The tree ring analysis of the 4,000 oak trees in the Strood causeway was dated between 684-702. The Strood is the only known Anglo-Saxon causeway would have been a major undertaking. A possible explanation for the causeway is that the King of the East Saxons, decided to adopt a monastic lifestyle and live on Mersea. The early Christians still followed the Celtic church and placed great importance on living in remote places, away from the sins of the world. St Cedd chose Bradwell and King Sarbbi chose Mersea and would have had the power to have a causeway built to the island.

THE RAY

The Ray is a channel from the Strood road crossing down towards the West Mersea yacht moorings. On a high spring tide the Strood road and saltings are often under water. All that remains above water is the 25-acre Ray Island. In the early Victorian period there was a small farm, cottage and barn on Ray Island. The island was divided into fields by hedges and it is claimed that there were traces of ploughing in some of the fields.

Ray Island was the setting for the novel 'Mehalah, A Story of the Salt Marshes,' first published in 1880. Sabine Baring Gould's story is of the intrigues surrounding Mehalah, a young

Judging the native oysters, on Packing Marsh Island, after the Mersea Dredging Match, 2009.

The houseboat *L'Esperance* at West Mersea. The houseboat colony at Mersea was started in the 1920s when old yachts were bought for their lead keels. They were then converted into houseboats.

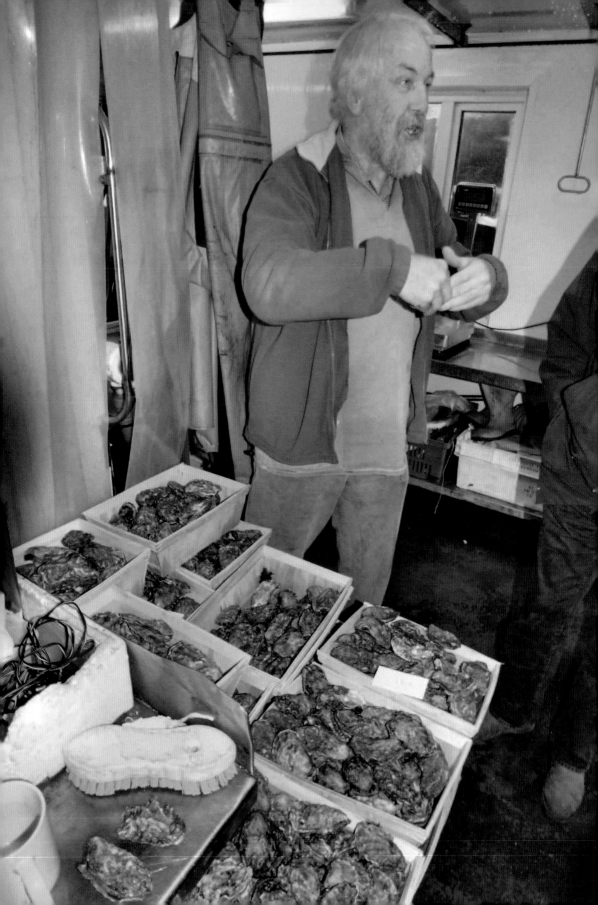

Richard Haward's oysters being cleaned on West Mersea water front.

Left: Richard Haward with gygigas oysters in the purification plant at the Company Shed, West Mersea, 2011.

girl who lived on Ray Island. Baring Gould wrote thirty novels and 'Mehalah' was his most successful.

At the head of the Ray, referred to as Peldon Creek, is the Shell Factory. Between 1920-24 smacks used to sail up here with oyster shells for grinding up into chicken grit. A bungalow was built on the site and in 1970 Johnny Milgate, who had trained at Wyatt's boatyard, bought the Shell Factory and opened it as a boat yard. Here he totally rebuilt the 35ft smack *Puritan*, and restored other smacks back to sail. In the 1980s the last two smacks working from West Mersea, with their sides thick with layers of tar, had been the *Puritan* and the *Our Boys*. Johnny Milgate also raced the smack *Peace* successfully.

WEST MERSEA

Mersea Island sits between the Rivers Colne and Blackwater with a labyrinth of tidal creeks on the inshore side. Mersea is divided into two villages, West Mersea known as 'The West' and East Mersea referred to as 'Down East.' West Mersea is not an easy place to visit by water or by road. There are very few available moorings and a noticeable lack of parking in the village. However the Creekside area is full of character. The Haward's Company Shed, fish restaurant, and other similar eating-places are great attractions to visitors.

It is said that a man with a horse plough laid out the street plan of West Mersea. It certainly was not the result of any recognized plan because it is a jumble of urban streets. The only real centre is around the church and here there is a good local museum that is open in the summer. The Mersea men are a friendly lot and it is cheerful place, a mixture of a deeply rooted local community and many newcomers.

Oysters thrive in the shallow creeks around

Looking across the Salcott Channel to Old Hall Marshes, 2009.

The Ship Dock at Abbott's Hall Saltings. The medieval river walls appear to have been low earth banks, but later, river walls were built up around alder stakes. The river walls are a vital part of the Essex heritage.

Mersea Island because of the mixture of salt and rainwater that creates the right nutrients for oyster growth. In the summer the rain on the saltings leaches the nutrients out into the creek for oysters to feed on. West Mersea is very proud of its long connection with oyster cultivation. Some claim this goes back to the Romans, but the Anglo-Saxons clearly realized that a system of rights was needed to safeguard oyster cultivation. The rights to cultivate the Mersea oyster grounds were part of the Manor of West Mersea, that were given by the Anglo-Saxon King, Edward the Confessor, to the Priory of St Ouen, in 1046.

The riverbed in much of the Blackwater is hard, which allows oysters to grow; they sink in soft mud and die. In time the hard oyster grounds on the bottom, in the creeks at Mersea, were dived into 'laying.' These individual layings were marked with 'withies.' where the oysters were 'fattened' after being dredged from the estuary. Before houses were built for residents who worked off The Island, oysters were the backbone of Mersea.

In the nineteenth century there were around 150 smacks working in and around the Blackwater. The oyster fishery declined after World War I and each hard winter reduced it further. Oysters can survive being frozen, but the ice lifts them off the bottom and carries them out into deep water. The hard winter of 1963 was a serious blow to the oyster industry and after this the Bonamia disease hit it. To keep the industry going the Pacific, or Rock 'gygigas' oysters were introduced. These oysters adjusted to the climate, and after about 1990 they spread out over the Blackwater.

The 'native' European (ostrea edulis) and gygigas oysters live happily side-by-side, but the gygigas can be eaten all the year round, while the natives can only be eaten when there is an R in the month. In the early 2000s the oyster fishery staged a modest recovery because of the Merseamen's very sustainable way of managing their native and gygigas oysters.

Mersea oysterman Richard 'Dick' Haward has the notebooks of his great-great-great-grandfather of 1792 when he sailed to London to sell his oysters. Dick has actively promoted the native oysters for his laying; some 400yards long, and also has acted as a merchant for several of the other oystermen. The Hawards opened the Company Shed, behind Punt Bay up near the old part of the village known as Mersea City, as a successful fish restaurant with a wonderful atmosphere.

David Gladwell dredges the European 'native' oysters in the River Blackwater in his dredging boat *Boy Steven II*, and these are re-laid in the warm shallow creeks for the start of the oyster season from September 1 until March. David Gladwell believed that the good oyster season of 2009 was due to the heavy rain in the early summer.

With powered craft, dredging oysters up from the creeks is fairly straightforward, but in the past the men had to do this in sailing smacks, and use their own strength to haul the dredge. In the 1930s the Merseamen were working in the last of their 20ft 'hauling and towing' skiffs. These were 'two ended' (pointed at both ends) and were worked, between two anchors, in the narrow creeks. The men anchored the skiff between two anchors in a creek, dropped a dredge over the stern and using the hand capstan in the skiff hauled it up to the other anchor. The dredge was then pulled up by hand, (hopefully) full of oysters. It was hard manual work but as the oystermen said 'the heaviest dredge is an empty dredge.'

As the hauling and towing skiffs needed two or three men, the one-man 'winkle brigs' were introduced in the 1920s. These were strongly built, often with grown frames, 16-18ft clinker, transom sterned, gaff sloops, Strong enough to take the weight of the oysters or winkles gathered on the foreshore. The West Mersea author Hervey Benham was accused of making up the name winkle brig, but the fishermen really did give them this name and the larger boats on the Colne were known as 'bumkins.' Fishermen have always been good at inventing better ways

The head of Old Hall Creek. This creek joins up with Tollesbury Fleet and passes The Nass into the Blackwater.

The last of the Tollesbury fleet of fishing smacks lying in the mud near Drake Brothers boatyard, at the head of Woodrolfe Creek, Tollesbury, in 1959. Fifty years later Google Earth aerial photographs tell a different story. The leisure boat era has produced the Marina at the head of the creek, while colonies of crabs have eroded the saltings with their burrows from the inside.

of fishing and giving imaginative terms for their boats and gear.

There were also skiffs used for unloading fishing boats of sprat or oysters. Clinker-built and very beamy, a 17footer could carry three and a half tons and be sculled by a single oar over the stern. They also had a 14inch wide 'mud keel' so that they could be slid over the mud, loaded. The last motor oyster skiff, working until 2002, was William Baker's *Native Oyster*.

In the Victorian period the term 'smack' meant a decked gaff-rigged fishing boat. This term appears to have come from the German 'smark,' the noise made by the old eighteenth century bluff-bowed boats smashing into the waves. By the end of the nineteenth century the Blackwater smacks evolved with low decks and counter sterns to make it easier to work the dredges. These fishing boats were very manoeuvrable in narrow channels. The Mersea and Colne smacks all carried the CK registration

(the first and last letters of Colchester Creek) although none operated from the town.

It was 1946 before the last West Mersea smack, the *Mersea Lass*, was fitted with an engine. However most of the smacks still had their sailing gear and in 1947 the annual smack race and winkle brig class for 'fisherman's open boats,' were revived in the West Mersea Regatta. Because they looked like Victorian yachts many people bought old fishing smacks and used them for pleasure sailing, but to start with they altered them to look like yachts and painted out the fishing numbers.

Then came Mike Frost, a Colchester dentist, who rowed around the smacks at Mersea and fell in love with the 30ft smack *Boadicea*, laying on her mooring in the Besom, a creek linking the Blackwater and Mersea Fleet. He was greatly attracted to the little dredging smack and he bought her in 1938. Unlike the other owners he kept her traditional working appearance and

The Sail Lofts at Tollesbury were built in about 1908 to store gear, off the big yachts, during the winter. The fishermen worked their smacks in winter, and went as paid crews on the great yachts in the summer.

Steve Hall of Tollesbury, opening the shrimp boiling copper on his 28ft Leigh shrimper *Victorious*, 2010. Steve had this shrimper restored back to the condition she had been in when she was built at Leigh in 1945. Summer shrimping was a major fishery on the Essex coast. In the 1950s there were seventeen boats shrimping from Tollesbury and twenty-one working from Harwich Harbour. In the 1930s the French had sent twenty boats over for shrimping. These had prisoners aboard and although they anchored off Shotley they never went ashore. The French also tried to work lobster pots on the West Rock and there were coal fights, with the Harwich men, who eventually removed all the French pots. The French boats came over for the last time in 1958. The demise of the shrimp fishery came as a result of the hard winter of 1963 when the wind blew hundreds of tonnes of dead shrimp on to the beaches in The Netherlands. Some Leigh boats continued on, but shrimp numbers never appear to have fully recovered.

went on fishing with her. It turned out that the *Boadicea* had been built at Maldon in 1808 and is the oldest craft still sailing in the British Isles. While many smacks were abandoned out on the saltings when the hulls wore out, Mike Frost was the first to totally rebuild his beloved *Boadicea*.

Other owners followed Mike Frost's example and by 2009 there were some sixty-two smacks and bawleys sailing in the Thames Estuary, almost all of them had been rebuilt, and kept in working appearance above deck. The enthusiasm for smack races, held from most Blackwater and Colne villages, has seen an increase in the sail area on the smacks. This competitive approach to racing has kept alive some of the spirit of

Victorian Essex. Essex men always enjoyed out-sailing their neighbours.

The old regattas had races for 'gunning punts' that had been used to raise a little income by shooting wildfowl out on the Blackwater in the winter. I am told that you can still get a punt gun, virtually a small cannon mounted in the bow of a punt, made in Mersea. Punt 'gunning' seems to have become a kind of 'black art' because of the powerful influence of the conservation lobby. A new narrow type of punt, based on the old gun punts, is used at Mersea just for racing.

In the sailing era Mersea smacks had just been worked in the Blackwater, but an enterprising fish merchant encouraged the Merseamen to buy

The oyster smacks *Hyacinth* and *Mayflower* in the Mersea Dredging Match, 2007. The smacks use the traditional method of going slowly sideways so that they can drag the dredges along the bottom and scoop up the oysters. The *Mayflower* was built by Aldous at Brightlingsea in 1887 and has been owned by Donald Rainbird since 1960 and kept to a working sail plan.

inshore fishing boats and work in the southern North Sea. By 1990 Mersea had thirty-five full time fishing boats, but by 2005 this was down to nine. In June 2009 the largest Mersea boat, the 14m *Nicola Anne*, was landing sole into a Dutch lorry, at Ipswich, to go to Italy. A year later Mersea had eight boats, two under 15meters and six under 10meters.

While Mersea Week is the height of the yacht racing calendar, the Round the Island Race, held in August, is also important. This race is about twelve miles around Mersea and can only be done at high water because the entrants have to sail up to the Strood and then drag their craft over the road during the race. This limits the race to small open boats and the record time, set up in 2002, was 56 minutes, set by John Ready and his crew in a Hurricane 5.9 catamaran.

SALCOTT CHANNEL

In the Roman period salt appears to have been made at Salcott-cum-Virley, at the head of the Salcott Channel, and the name Salcott (pronounced 'Sawc't') literally means 'cottage where the salt is stored.'

On November 2nd, 2002, the *East Anglian Daily Times* reported that the Essex Wildlife Trust had made their first breach in the river at Abbots Hall Farm, Great Wigborough. The Essex Wildlife Trust had bought the 700 acre Abbots Hall with a £1m legacy and applied to flood the low-lying ground. The report said that the Government Minister present beamed as the tide swept in across the stubble of the last year's barley. In our urban society the importance of farmland is totally forgotten, and also the old maxim that at any time anarchy is only ever nine meals away.

Later the Essex Wildlife Trust made five

Maldon Oyster's 'rake and sack' oyster production, on Goldhanger Beach, 2011.

more breaks and flooded 120 acres. What was actually happening was that the amount of water going up and down the Salcott Channel was increasing and this was causing more erosion further down the creek. Trying to create saltings by flooding arable land is very slow at the best and can take up to two hundred years. For new saltings to grow up, silt has to be torn off the existing channel, causing more erosion. Basically managed alignment is just moving silt from one place to another and in the long-term it does not increase the amount of bird habitat.

The Ship Dock (not Ship Lock) at Abbots Hall Farm is a curious walled in island outside the river wall. It could have been a place where 'ships' (sheep) were housed at high tide when they were grazing the saltings, or perhaps even a dry area to store hay and straw before it was shipped off to London.

The oyster cultivators at West Mersea strongly objected to the flooding of Abbots Hall because in 1992, further up the Salcott Channel, a landowner had been given permission to flood fresh water marshes and this appears to have

The 33ft smack *Polly*, under reefed sail, with the Bradwell Power Station in the background, 2009. The *Polly*, built by Howard at Maldon in 1889, was one of the smaller smacks that were used for dredging and fishing in the Blackwater.

brought silt down the creek.

Before World War I barges such as *Lord Warden* went right up to the Salcott church, and a few even up to the 'White Hart,' to load stack freights. However the very narrow channel at the head of the creek was walled off to save the expense of maintaining a long area of river wall.

OLD HALL CREEK

There are some fifty-eight creeks on the Blackwater, some little more than gullies in the mud, but Tollesbury cuts right into the side of rural Essex. At the very head of Tollesbury Fleet is Old Hall Creek. In the eighteenth century the remote Old Hall quay was a favourite haunt for smugglers, but the Revenue men once seized 210 tubs of Dutch geneva gin here and took it to Colchester in two wagons.

Old Hall's Ship-Ahoy Quay used to be the main place for barge traffic for the area. In about 1850 fifty people lived here and it had its own pub, the 'Hoy Inn.' A hoy was a craft that ran a regular service between two ports. Before the railways most communities around the Thames

The main house on Osea Island

Estuary had a vessel running a regular packet and passenger Hoy service to a particular wharf in the Pool of London.

Between Tollesbury Fleet and the Salcott Channel are the Old Hall Marshes. In the 1890s over 2000 sheep grazed on Old Hall Marshes and adjoining saltings. These famous wildfowling marshes have 9kms of river wall around them. In 1949 James Wentworth Day wrote with enthusiasm about how 'Crawley' de Crespigny had killed up to three hundred duck, with six fellow 'guns,' at the opening of the wildfowling season on August 8th. When Wentworth Day rented the Old Hall marshes for shooting, he hired a smack and anchored for the night near Cob Island, in the middle of Tollesbury Fleet. I understand the excitement that Wentworth Day and his friends had when they set off in a boat, at dawn, to land on the saltings and shoot the incoming duck. However, a more positive form of preservation has been the RSPB taking over the marsh for conservation.

The top of Tollesbury Fleet was walled off in 1751 and this remained good food-producing land until 1995. In March of that year I was one of a party that went to view an 80m hole

acknowledged to have been a mistake, monitoring at Tollesbury stopped so that the flooding policy was not put into question. As the marshes were low-lying they had just turned into a lagoon, while the extra water roaring in and out of the gap had altered the navigation channel. The problem is that this sort of action is often irreversible because the water lapping at the back the river wall erodes it away, making it extremely expensive to reclaim.

TOLLESBURY

Tollesbury is a large village standing amongst the green fields of the rich East Essex farmland, with little hint of the sea. In the distance is the River Blackwater with Tollesbury Fleet running inland from Mersea Quarters. Tollesbury has always been a place on its own, slightly cut off from the rest of Essex.

There is a wonderful, totally flat, expanse of saltings between Tollesbury and West Mersea that are excellent coastal bird habitat. The great Essex marshes have grown, over the centuries, because of the steadily rising sea level. The saltings are always at the mean high water level and continue to rise with sea levels.

The problem with Tollesbury Fleet is that it has a very shallow patch near the Shingle head Point, barely a few feet of water at low tide. Above this the Fleet divides into a North and South channel, either side of Great Cob Island. North channel goes up to Old Hall Creek while on the South channel, just after the Leavings, where the smacks were based, Woodrolfe Creek goes up to Tollesbury.

Woodrolfe Creek used to be called 'Wood-Up Creek' by the older generation of fishermen, possibly because timber ships used to come up here. This name was corrupted into Woodrolfe Creek and became the maritime centre of Tollesbury Creek. Drake is listed as being a shipwright at Old Hall and in about 1865 the Drakes built a granary on silts at Woodrolfe Creek and gradually the trade switched there. William Frost had the boomies *James Bowles*,

that English Nature had made in the river wall. This was the first time that English Nature had received permission to break down river defences. The party stood in silence while a young man from English Nature spoke with missionary zeal about the fact that, by allowing the tide to flow on this land, new saltings would be created in a few years, which would be habitat for brent geese. The mood in our party was of dismay and anger. We all felt very betrayed by the very people we looked to for countryside preservation.

Fifteen years later this flooding was

The *Mary, Mayfly* and *Martha II* locking into the Basin, after the Heybridge Regatta Smack Race, 2005. There were some sixty-eight Essex smacks afloat in 2010. The fishing registration letters MN is for Maldon, and CK for Colchester Creek; the first and last letters of the area where they used to be based.

Darnet and the *Empress of India* bringing coal up to Woodrolfe Hard and Fisher had the sprittie barge *Tollesbury*, brand new in 1901, for local work.

At the mouth of the Blackwater there is a 'common ground' open for anyone to dredge oysters. Up river from this, between West Mersea and Stone Point, only the Tollesbury and Mersea Company can dredge, and further up the Maldon Oyster Company have grounds. In the past the smackmen had poached each other's oysters to such an extent that it all evened out in the end.

In 1894 about forty Blackwater smacks were dredging for 'culch' (old oyster shells used to attract oyster sprat) on the common ground when four smacks turned up from Burnham and also started dredging. Legally the Burnham men were entitled to work the common ground, but the Blackwater men were furious that 'foreigners' were dredging on 'common ground' that they regarded as being exclusive to them.

The Tollesbury men tried to intimidate the Burnham men by sailing very close, but they didn't go away. After this the strongest Blackwater men boarded four of the Tollesbury smacks and hid in the hold with shovels. When the Burnham smacks had clearly filled their holds the Tollesbury smacks sailed alongside and the men jumped out of the holds shouting, and boarded the Burnham smacks. They then shovelled the Burnham smacks day's 'culch' back into the Blackwater. One Burnham smack got away, but the others brought a charge of 'piracy' against the Blackwater men. The case held in Chelmsford was the last case of piracy heard in British waters, but the Tollesbury and Mersea men were acquitted.

The smackmen working from the Leavings in the South channel used to land on the hard and then had a long walk back to the village. In 1907 the Kelvedon & Tollesbury Light

Railway Company opened a railway line across Tollesbury Wick Marshes to a new pier on the River Blackwater near Mill Creek. The new Pier was to attract grand yachts, and there was even a hope of starting a passenger service to Europe, However the open Blackwater was too exposed as a yacht anchorage. The pier stopped operating as a commercial venture in 1921. Most of it was pulled down in 1940 and the last remains went in 1951.

In 1902 a new company, the Tollesbury Yacht Berthing Company tried to develop Tollesbury at Woodrolfe Hard for yachts of up to 300 tons. The wooden Sail Lofts on silts, beside Woodrolfe Hard, were built to store yacht gear during the winter. Although this venture did not live up to the high hopes of their promoters they did stimulate the Tollesbury men into greater maritime enterprises. Tollesbury blossomed as a rival to the older established centres of Rowhedge, Wivenhoe and Brightlingsea as a fishing and yachting centre. The men went fishing for sprat in their smacks in the winter and in the summer they shipped on the grand yachts as paid 'hands', although some stayed at home to go shrimping in their smacks, and had boilers fitted for cooking the shrimp.

In 1921 the Tollesbury Smack Race was revived and held from the pier. The following year a Tollesbury smack was the first to be fitted with an engine, a 15hp Kelvin, and within a few years all the smacks from Brightlingsea, Wivenhoe and Rowhedge had engines. These low-powered engines ended total reliance on the wind and after this most smacks just had a cut down mainsail and foresail, but they continued doing the same form of fishing. One of the early engines did not last very long as the crew were unaware that the oil had to be checked as well as the fuel!

In the 1930s there were still 150 fishermen living in Tollesbury, but many of these were going away in the summer as paid hands on large yachts. However 'real yachting' was dying out and the fishing declining. The Tollesbury fishermen had a reputation for being rather bold and searched all over the Thames estuary for fish, but the fleet slowly declined.

In the 1950s many Colne and Blackwater fishermen were still working motorized smacks that their grandfathers' had had built. In 1970 Tollesbury was down to seven men working five boats. These old-timers kept going as long as they could. The smack *Iris Mary* was dredging oysters at Tollesbury under power until 1985. John 'Southerly' Frost worked the 45ft smack *Varuna*, bought new by his father in 1895, until 1975 and this smack went on to be the last one fishing in Essex. However, after this the Rigbys operated powered fishing boats from Tollesbury.

Tollesbury Yacht Harbour was dug when John Goldie and the boatbuilder Jack Waterhouse bought Drake Bros yard and five acres of saltings. The gullies and rills were dammed up and 80,000 tons of soil excavated to form the basin. On the lowest neap tide in September 1970 the last soil was removed, allowing the incoming tide to come roaring in to fill the basin. Now known as Tollesbury Marina, the basin can berth 200 yachts.

Sir Alex Rose opened the Tollesbury Cruising Club, beside the Marina, in 1971. Tollesbury Sailing Club had been started in 1936 and had a Club House opposite the Ibex Sail Loft. This loft had probably been built in the 1890s as a winter store for the gear of the steam yacht *Ibex*. Gayle Heard, whose father had successfully skippered the large racing yachts, opened this loft to become North Sea Sails. When Gayle retired Steve Hall, a Wivenhoe man trained at Brightlingsea, continued traditional sail making here.

The fifty-two flats of Woodrolfe Park were built in 1972 as holiday homes, but increasingly people have moved in to live here full time. When Woodrolfe Park was built, a wooden building was moved over the river wall on rollers to a new site beside Woodrolfe Hard. This had been the Cranfield & Carter sail loft, but in 1980 Trevor 'Mouse' Green, who had bought Frost & Drake, started his own boat building and repair yard here.

The Blackwater Barge Match, 2009. There had been annual barge races at Maldon until 1936 and the race was revived in 1962.

Tollesbury has the Salt Pool, a public swimming pool filled with seawater by the tide. These were once common; there were seawater pools at Leigh, Maldon, Mistley, Woodbridge and Orford. All now closed, while Tollesbury's pool with its sandy beach, opened in 1908, has remained popular. It has a wonderful notice saying that if more that a thousand people are in the pool no more should enter, but it does not say who does the counting!

Across the road from the Salt Pool and Mouse's shed is Bonton creek, at the head of Woodrolfe Creek. After Bonton Creek boatyard there is a wide expanse of salting stretching out to the main Tollesbury Creek. These saltings belong to Fellowship Afloat, an organization devoted to getting young people on the water for recreation. In about 1967 Fellowship Afloat bought the *Memory*, a barge regarded by some as being the finest that Cann of Harwich had ever built, They used her as a clubhouse until she was replaced by the lightship. Fellowship Afloat have called Tollesbury 'Heaven on Earth,' which it

might just be, because the tide is out most of the time and it seems a very peaceful place.

GOLDHANGER

Goldhanger Creek leads off from the main channel of the Blackwater, behind Osea Island, some two miles, up to the village. Here there is a hard foreshore and two posts, one recently damaged, where stackie barges used to load. There are a few boats kept here, but there is only water here about an hour and a half each side of high water.

In 1991 Ron Hall, of Maldon, lost an anchor on the mud flats near Cooper Creek, at the entrance of Goldhanger Creek, and when he went back to look for it at low tide, he discovered rows and rows of wooden post stumps on the mud flats. After extensive research these were identified as being the remains of medieval fish traps and this led on to the discovery of further fish traps in St Lawrence Bay, the Nass at Mersea, St Peter's Point and Foulness, which are

The sailing barge *Mirosa*, built by Howard at Maldon in 1892, off Osea Island. Although a fast sailer, this barge has a straight deck line and the low sides of a stackie barge. She also has a low bow, that helps to prevent windage on the bow and doesn't stop her from turning about, when tacking up narrow channels.

dated between 940-990.

Because there is a hard beach on Goldhanger Creek, Val Devall's Maldon Oysters started cultivating oysters here, in about 1963. The oysters lay on the foreshore and were picked up by hand. Later the French system was introduced where by oysters were fattened in bags on racks. These are harvested with the help of a tractor, at low water, but escapees are dredged up, at high tide, by a boat from Mersea. The oysters are then taken to a purification, grading and packing plant in Cock Clarks, which is the largest oyster packing plant in the United Kingdom. It must take tough men to work out on the bleak beach at Goldhanger in the middle of the winter, but they gather oysters here and seem to enjoy the freedom of working in the fresh air.

OSEA ISLAND

The 330-acre Osea Island is linked to Heybridge by a causeway that floods at high tide. The causeway is submerged for eight out of every twelve hours of tides. On neap tides the water can remain over the causeway as long as sixteen hours.

The Romans made salt on Osea and probably built the first causeway. After 1066 two men lived on the island looking after sheep. The oldest house on Osea was built in 1620 and the island always seems to have been run as one farm. In the Victorian period Osea had its own Post Office, but in the 1860s the postman, and his horse and cart, got caught by the tide on the causeway, and were swept away.

Frederick Charrington's wealth came from the family brewing business, but when he saw a drunken man staggering out of one of their pubs, he decided to tackle the problem of alcoholism. He bought Osea Island in 1903 and built the Mansion House, the pier, chapel and sanatorium as a home for 'gentlemen inebriates.' The sanatorium was one of the first all concrete buildings constructed, and in 1992 this was converted to flats and called Charrington House.

According to local legend, Charrington's

After the 2010 Barge Match the 'spritty' barge *Edme* touched her bow on the mud, so that the flood tide would turn her round to come alongside the Hythe Quay, Maldon. The *Edme* and *Mirosa* are still sailed without engines and are kept in a traditional appearance.

good intentions were rather scuppered because the Maldon fishermen had a roaring trade smuggling booze on to the island. The bottles were left pegged to the foreshore. During both World Wars I and II Osea became a top secret Naval base for high speed craft. Two servicemen based on Osea won the VC for a motor torpedo boat raid on German ports. An unsuccessful attack on the Russian fleet at St Petersburg was also launched from here. The idea had been to prevent the warships from falling into Communist hands.

When David and Michael Cole bought Osea in 1966, David was the first owner of the island to actually live there. In 1976 David Cole sold Osea to Cambridge University, but in 1984 he bought it back again. Most of the stores needed for the island were brought down river by boat from Heybridge Basin.

Russell Large worked for David Cole, and lived on Osea for sixteen years, He said it was a wonderful place to live, once you had got used to planning your life around the times when the causeway was open. During Russell's time on Osea, about half a dozen cars had got caught by the rising tide and were abandoned.

In 2007 David Cole sold Osea Island, but kept the Captain's House on the point, and a barn. The new owner developed Osea as a drug rehabilitation centre, which meant that the permanent population of fifteen had to leave. The last resident to go, and probably the most reluctant, was Den Phillips, the renowned Maldon photographer, who had lived there for thirty years.

HEYBRIDGE

Heybridge Creek, opposite Maldon, was the original course of the River Blackwater where the Chelmer joined the Blackwater. When the Chelmer and Blackwater Navigation was built in 1793 the main stream was diverted away from the creek down a new cut to reach the Blackwater at the new village of Heybridge

Drawing by Barry Pearce of 'Slosher' Wright, one of the bargemen and fishermen who, in the 1950s, still used to gather down at the bench on the Bath Wall. Here the Claydons, Pitts, Handleys, Taylors, Tracys, Quilters and others used to gather to exchange stories and gossip in the 'Bath Wall Parliament.' In the Victorian period Ben Handley had a tin shed, the Bath House, where visitors came for saltwater bathing. In 1905 the Marine Lake was created for the public to swim in. After a tragedy, the Marine Lake was altered to become a wild life feature.

a missionary sent there were the soles of his boots.

Heybridge became the centre for two large timber importers. Sadds had a large timber yard just above Heybridge Creek and Browns of Chelmsford imported timber through Heybridge Basin. Both companies had timber ships anchored off Osea Island and the timber was taken up river by barge. Brown's off-loaded their timber barges into 30ton barges in Heybridge Basin, and these were towed up to Chelmsford by horses. In 1965 the lock gates at Heybridge were enlarged so that Baltic timber ships could go straight in. The last timber ship into Heybridge was the Danish *Conland*, in 1971.

The Basin Regatta, at Heybridge, in the Basin Reach is an old style event for the local community with races for yachts, smacks, rowing races and the greasy pole. The Basin Regatta probably started in about 1820 and continued until about 1938, but was revived in 1977. E.H. Bentall had his famous racing yacht *Jullanar* built in Heybridge Basin in 1874. He was a keen supporter of the Regatta and also founder and Commodore of the Blackwater Sailing Club.

Basin. A weir was built at Bee Leigh Abbey and the excess fresh water from the River Chelmer was diverted through a new cut at Fullbridge, Maldon. The old silted-up course of the river became Heybridge Creek and has been used by 'Noddy' Cardy as a place to store lighters.

Heybridge Basin took trade away from the quays at Maldon and there was over a century of bitter rivalry between the two ports, at the head of the Blackwater. The gangs of men from rival ports used to meet and fight. The Maldon people claimed that the 'Basiners,' the Chaneys, Stebbens, Woodcrafts and Quilters, were cannibals and all that was ever found of

The first Blackwater Sailing Club clubhouse, built in about 1910, was a small wooden hut behind the river wall at the creek mouth, on the site of a salt works that had closed in 1825. The barge wharf, where stackie barges loaded, was incorporated into the sailing club. In the second half of the twentieth century leisure boating took over the river and the Blackwater Sailing Club blossomed, with a fine new clubhouse and many more facilities.

There had been a tide mill in this area and Saltcote Mill, at the head of the creek, was built in about 1895 as a maltings. Mill Beach Hotel on the riverfront was also built about the same time. John Howard built the barge *Saltcote Belle* (named after farmer Gower's high milk yielding cow) at Maldon, in 1895. This barge used to be loaded with malt for London at the well-maintained quay at the head of the creek. On small, 'neap' tides, the *Saltcote Belle* was loaded with malt in Heybridge Basin. The last sailing barge up to the mill with a cargo appears to have been the *Centaur* in 1952. The quay has since been filled in, while Saltcote Mill has been converted to flats.

MALDON

Maldon is famous for salt, barges and mud. The best way to see Maldon is to come up river on an early summer's morning. The Blackwater is a wide estuary, but after Osea it starts to get narrower and there ahead are the rooves of Maldon, sitting on a hilltop. Rounding the final Herring Point (named after a farmer not the

fish) the barges become visible, lying against the Hythe Quay and the Church above guarding over them.

Maldon still has boatyards, but at one time there were 'wooden walls' built here for the Royal Navy. The largest of these was the 500tonner, 50gun 4th rater *Jersey*, launched by Starline in 1654 from the Shipways, just up river from the Hythe Quay and the Town Hard. Later brigs and schooners were built here and in the Victorian era there was a steady demand for sailing barges, smacks and a few yachts. The first sailing barge built here was the *Landford*, launched in 1796, but there were already twenty-seven sailing barges owned in Maldon.

The most renowned of the Blackwater barge builders was John Howard who, between the *Surprise* in 1879, and the *Defender* in 1900, built twenty-four barges, all combining handsome hulls with good sailing abilities. He also built barge yachts, smacks and yachts. Howard had the Shipways, at the bottom of North Street. The

'marine railway' (slipway) went up to the V in the road.

Farming was the major industry around the Blackwater so most of Howard's barges were 'stackies,' taking hay, straw and mangolds for the London street horses and cows in barns and returning with muck. The 'stackie' barges had to have beamy hulls because they sailed with a stack of straw half way up the main mast. The skipper, standing at the wheel aft, could not see where he was going and had to be guided by the mate standing on top of the stack. The stack had to be lashed down well and covered with a 'cloth', but even then, after a rough trip down the Swin, stackies sometimes arrived in the Thames with all, or part of their stack, having vanished overboard.

Some of Howard's barges have survived, the *Mermaid* (1888) and the *Violet* (1889) are in a poor shape as houseboats. The *Ethel Maud* (1889) is being rebuilt and *Mirosa* (1892) is still sailing. The 80ft *Ethel Maud* was built for Clem Parker,

Paul Jefferies, skipper-owner of the Topsail Charter's mulie barge *Hydrogen*, 2007.

a Bradwell farmer who had a fleet of barges taking hay and straw to London and in 1910 she was sold to Keeble, at Maldon. The *Ethel Maud* spent seventy-three years carrying cargoes into the Blackwater, first in the 'stackie' trade and when this faded out in the 1920s, she was sold to the millers, Green Bros.

Many barges were built from half models, but Howard had designed his craft on paper and was always trying something new. In 1900 Howard was asked to build a shallow draft yacht, carrying a punt on deck, for wild fowling in the winter. He designed the 30ft centreboard yacht *Eider Duck*, and although not fast, she fulfilled the owner's needs. However, due to cash flow problems, Howard's yard was closed down and Cook and Woodward took on the order and built the *Eider Duck*.

When the hay and straw merchant, Keeble, wanted a barge built for the stackie trade he asked Walter Cook to build the barge *Dawn*, on the old Hedgecoe shipyard site, just down river from the Hythe. Cook, with his brother-in-law Woodward, had worked for Howard as shipwrights, and used his idea of having iron deck beams in a wooden barge. To get the *Dawn* launched in 1897 the river wall had to be dug away and it then took two days to get her into the water. Cook and Woodward went on to build the *Lord Roberts* (1900) and the *British King* (1901) but their barges lacked the grace and speed of their former master's barges. The *Dawn* had to be rebuilt at Walter Cooks & Son in 1928 because the muck cargoes had started to make her hull rot.

The Shipway was taken over by Dan Webb and Feesey who built the Blackwater sloops and other small wooden yachts. Between 1957-59 John Scarlett, with advice from Jack Feesey, built his 22ft yacht *Essex Melody* to his own design. John Scarlett, an academic electronic engineer at Marconi, worked at the Baddow research site, with his own 'hut,' on Mercury delay lines, an essential component of early computers.

John loved the theory of boating, rather than actually sailing, but became the leading figure in starting the Old Gaffers Association. After the Maldon Smack Race was revived in 1956 the smack *Fly* kept winning because her owner, dentist Roy Clarkson, could afford new sails. The other owners, who had sailing smacks with old working sails, decided this was 'cheating.'

Passions ran high, as they often do in smack racing circles, and Roy Clarkson said he would not race with the smacks again. Roy persuaded John Scarlett to organize a race just for 'gaff rigged boats.' After the first Old Gaffers Race on the River Blackwater in 1963 John Scarlett put tremendous energy in to being Secretary of the new Old Gaffers Association. He had a room in his bungalow on Fambridge Road where he worked away doing OGA administration. John fell out dramatically with Roy when the *Fly* didn't win the early races.

The first fibreglass hulled yachts had appeared on the East Coast in the late 1950s and it was obvious that great changes were about to happen. Given Maldon's enthusiasm for barges and smacks it is not surprising that the OGA should have started here. Maldon became the stronghold of good shipwrights working with wooden hulls. At the Downs Road yard Brian Kennell and a team of shipwrights completed a series of 'rebuilds.' These are actually new hulls built on the exact lines of the original hulls that were dismantled as the work progressed. The theory is that if a hull occupies exactly the same air space as the original hull, it is the same craft. These were major wooden hulls such as Richard Titchener's 44ft smack *Sallie*, originally built by Aldous in 1907, which was finished in 1989 and the 44ft *My Alice* being worked on in 1995.

The spritsail barge is a brilliant piece of Victorian technology for moving cargo cheaply, that should have faded out when the diesel engines came in, but instead a whole new era, funded by 'charter' work, began. At Maldon the custom had been that a barge could lay free of charge between cargoes at the Hythe Quay. Although they got charged later on, the free quay drew barges to Maldon in the early 1960s and they began to pay their way running 'charter'

trips with passengers. Two young skippers, John Fairbrother and Peter Light, who had been totally dedicated to keeping the barges trading under sail as long as possible, then switched their enthusiasm to getting charter barges going. Fred Cooper had skippered the *Marjorie* in the first charter venture in 1962. Another former trading barge skipper Jim Lawrence came back to skipper the *Marjorie* in the summer. Because he needed work in the winter he made a new fores'l for the barge and this progressed into the well-known Brightlingsea sail loft of James Lawrence Sailmakers.

During the trading barge era Maldon was simply another barge port, but charter work made this tidal port the centre of barges in the Thames Estuary. The most successful of the Maldon charter barge operators has been Topsail Charters, started by Paul Jefferies and Stephanie Valentine in 1987 as an agency to book trips on barges, but in 1992 they bought the big wooden *Hydrogen* then the steel *Thistle* and the steel *Reminder* and remained agent for two other barges. Once barges came up river at high tide loaded almost down to the deck with a cargo, but in the revival era they come up at high water, in the summer, with their decks covered in passengers returning from a day out on the river.

The Maldon smacks were kept on the beach below Hythe Quay. This area is known as the Bath Wall because, in the Victorian period, there was male and female bathing here, separated for modesty, by a high fence. Essex smacks had all been transom sterned (nothing to do with the later bawleys) and Maldon men kept their transoms; long after the rest of the Essex smackmen who had been influenced, by the grand yachts, into having graceful counter sterns.

The Maldon smacks originally went fishing down the 'Pant' (the old name for the river Blackwater) and occasionally went as far afield as Manningtree or Walton Backwaters, but mostly they left Bath Wall at high tide and went down river on the ebb. They then dredged for oysters or fished and returned to Maldon on the next

Walter Linnet's cottage, on Sale's Point, Bradwell, overlooks the entrance to the River Blackwater.

high tide. Some of the early smacks had wet wells to keep the oysters alive, and on Saturdays they sailed to West Mersea and sold their oysters to the merchants there. In 1890 there were seventy men and boys oyster dredging from Maldon and Mike Emmett was the last one when he gave up in 1995, to pursue his wandering life sailing, and writing books.

Some fishing families had come around from the Thames, because the Thames was getting polluted. 'Alfa' Pitt's family had originally worked from Greenhithe, but they had loaded their smack up with furniture and sailed around to Maldon. As well as being a fisherman Alfa's father had been the 'huffler,' working barges up Heybridge Creek. The Maldon fishermen also worked at Osea or in the Basin Reach, unloading the timber ships.

The last men working a smack under sail in the Blackwater were 84-year old Ernie Pitt and his 77-year old brother, in 1956. The younger brother fell overboard off Bradwell, but managed to get back aboard and after this Ernie said 'we had better get rid of the little smack a' fore she gets rid of us' and the *Polly* was sold to become a yacht.

The River Blackwater has wide areas of mud flats below the saltings where water is left on the falling tide. These shallow pools evaporate and salt is left, and on high spring tides this salt is swept up river making the Blackwater one of the saltiest rivers in the country. Even in the Bronze Age salt water was being boiled along the rivers edge, for food preservation, which left the areas known as the Red Hills.

The Domesday Book recorded salt making at Maldon and there was a salt works here in 1777. The present salt works, just below Fullbridge, has been there since 1882. In 1894 Maldon was one of the only places left in Britain where sea salt was produced. The Maldon Crystal Salt Company is a modern factory, but still collects river water into holding tanks on spring tides and then the water is boiled off in pans leaving the sea salt.

It is not just salt that comes up the Blackwater, there is silt too. At one time the fresh water coming down from the River Chelmer kept the quays clear, but as more water has been taken out for human use, the silt began to block up the Maldon quays. In 2002 the mud dredged up was put on the decaying saltings opposite Maldon Promenade and this has been reported as being a great success. This is a considerably more sensible way of creating more new saltings as bird habitat than flooding land. It does less damage to the environment and is far cheaper.

The Maldon Mud Race is a dash across the River Blackwater that is held at low tide just after Christmas. The Race is aimed at raising money for charity and was started in 1973 when there was a dare made in the 'Queen's Head' for someone to cross over in the mud, dressed in a full tuxedo, and serve a meal on the other side. This was carried out and the following year twenty people took part and this race ended with the drinking of a pint of beer. The pint of beer was dropped, but the race was held annually in front of the 'Queen's Head' until 1989. Maldon Carnival restarted the race between 1998 and 2000, but it was stopped because of Health and Safety regulations. The Lions and Rotary clubs restarted the race lower down the river in 2002.

Running through the soft mud and wading through the fast flowing tidal stream is hard work, but the winner usually takes about five minutes while the mud-covered stragglers take about half an hour. By 2009 people were coming from all over the world to take part and about 250 people fought their way across the Blackwater. The mud race was cancelled in 2010 because there was 3inches of ice on the mud, and moved to Easter. Where there is mud, there is life.

NORTHEY ISLAND

The Northey Island is linked to the mainland by a causeway that is covered at high tide. This causeway is believed to have been the site of the Battle of Maldon in 991. An invading Viking army camped on Northey and the Anglo-Saxon Earl Brithnoth brought an army down to repel the Vikings. There was an Anglo-Saxon poem about the Battle of Maldon and although the original was destroyed in a fire at Westminster in 1721, a copy had been made. According to the poem the Vikings said they could not fight unless they were allowed to go across the causeway. Brithnoth allowed them on to the mainland

St Peter's on the Wall, at Bradwell. This was built by St Cedd in about 654, when he brought Christianity to the kingdom of the East Saxons. Because it is a very early church St Peter's is given the same status as a Cathedral and permission to have a wedding there has to be given by the Archbishop of Canterbury.

where they promptly destroyed his army and killed him. A statue of Brithnoth stands on the end of the Promenade at Maldon, challenging anyone coming up river.

Northey became a marshland farm, but most the river walls were breached in 1887 destroying the farm's viability. In 1978 Northey was given to the National Trust, but there is a limited public access.

Just down river is Lawling Creek and there was a barge wharf here at Brick House Farm. Leading off Lawling Creek is the smaller Maylandsea Creek that leads up to the boatyard. This area once had orchards but in the 1920s a developer sold off the area in plots as 'Maylandsea Bay.' Most of the original chalets have been replaced with houses, and lower down the Blackwater much the same has happened at Stone Point.

The countryside around St Lawrence Bay is neat fields and the farm buildings and houses are orderly and practical. The villages and numerous caravan parks are also neat and tidy.

BRADWELL-ON-SEA

I first heard of Bradwell from Arthur Hunt, who I used to help when I was still at school. Arthur was skipper of the 31ft yacht *Genesta*, built by W. King & Sons at Burnham in 1926, and I helped him move this yacht around. This suited us both, I was able to go afloat and Arthur got someone he could trust at the tiller. My reward was being regaled with tales about the coast before World War I, down in the cabin at the end of the day.

Arthur had 'run away to sea' on a boomie barge, but then went on to be mate on the *Dover Castle*, owned by Clem Parker of Bradwell. Clem, a farmer, had some smart barges in the 'stackie' trade taking hay and straw to London and returning with muck. They loaded at nearby farms and Hervey Benham recorded that Parker's barges loaded at 'Deal Hall, Pigeon Dock and the Hoo Outfall round the great wall of Bradwell.'

The skipper of the *Dover Castle* went off sick

and Clem asked Arthur to skipper the barge, which he did. One day they were lying at Bradwell Quay when Clem Parker came down to the Quay on his white horse and said 'your skipper is coming back and you are to go back as mate again.'

Arthur said he was now a skipper and demanded to take one of the other barges. Clem, a man who always knew his mind, said that it was for him to decide who sailed his barges. Arthur packed his sea bag and left Parker and barges.

Years later Arthur went back into Bradwell in the *Genesta* and he met Clem on the quay. By then the old man had sold his barges. The two men chatted happily about the barges and Clem said 'we were both young and hot headed then.'

Bradwell-on-Sea is an inland village at the end of a point between the River Blackwater and the Dengie Flats. Although Bradwell appears remote it has two public houses, the 'King's Head' and 'Cricketers,' and is a much visited area with caravan parks. The three places of interest on the coast are Bradwell Waterside, a hamlet with the old barge quay and a modern marina. Bradwell nuclear power station dominates the entrance of the River Blackwater. Just around the point there is the Othona Christian centre with St Peter's on the Wall chapel, and Walter Linnet's Cottage, that is used by the Essex Wildlife Trust to monitor birds out on the salting and around Gunner's Creek.

Walter Linnet appears to have been Essex's last professional wildfowler, but he once told a sporting wildfowler 'if you have a pound in your pocket you don't need to shoot the duck.' The little tarred cottage where he lived appears to have originally been a Napoleonic War signal station. This was one of a number of cottages that were prefabricated at Chatham and put up at lookout points to watch out for a French invasion.

Chapter Five

THE ESTUARY COAST

River Crouch, Roach Islands and Thames Mouth

NORTH FAMBRIDGE
BRIDGE MARSH ISLAND
BURNHAM ON CROUCH
BATTLEBRIDGE
WALLASEA
PAGLESHAM EAST END
FOULNESS
POTTON ISLAND
BARLING
LITTLE WAKERING
GREAT WAKERING
LEIGH ON SEA
SOUTHEND ON SEA
CANVEY ISLAND
TWO TREE ISLAND
RIVER CROUCH
ROACH ISLANDS
THAMES MOUTH

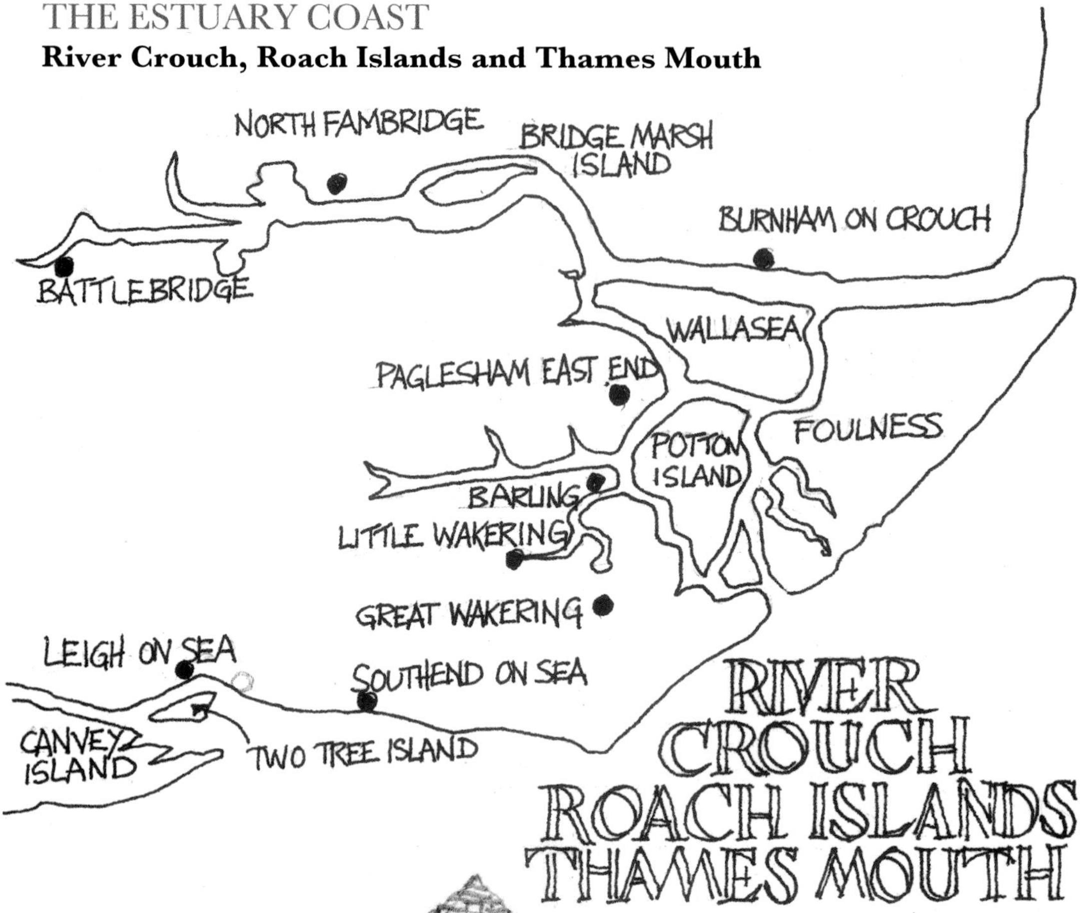

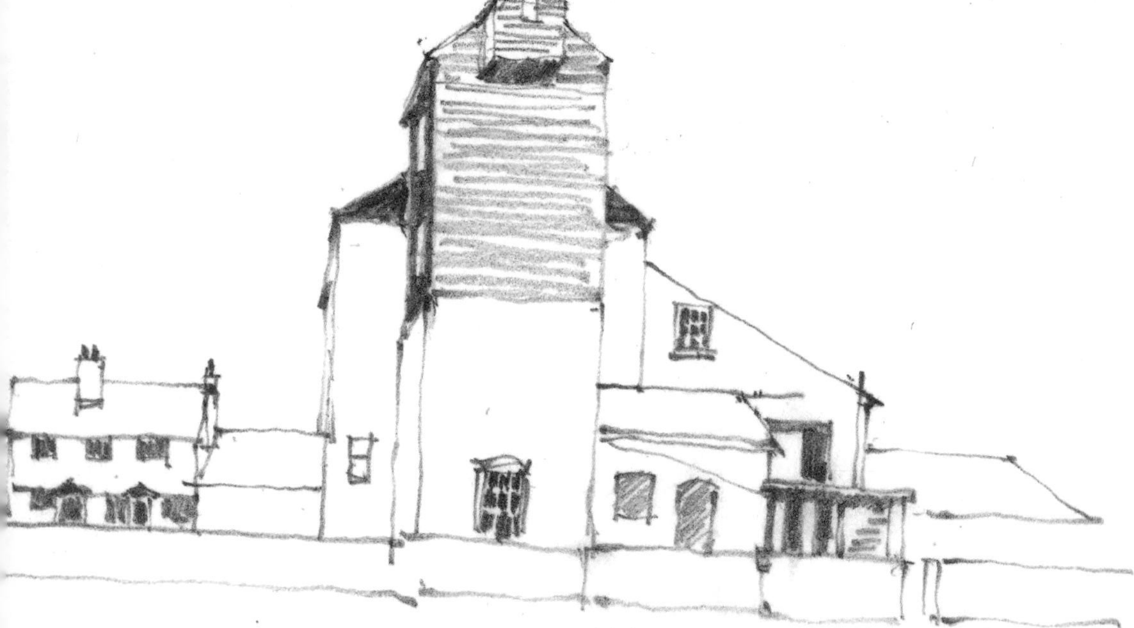

DENGIE COAST

Although Dengie is only a small parish, well back from the sea, it has given its name to the Hundred. When the railway reached Southminster that village grew to dominate the countryside overlooking the Dengie and Burnham marshes. The whole Dengie Marsh coast, from Sales Point at Bradwell down to the River Crouch, is very good farmland where quality wheat is grown. While the Blackwater saltings are badly damaged by crabs the Dengie saltings, which are open to the sea, are sandy and don't seem to have been attacked by crabs.

The low coast from the Blackwater to Shoeburyness is the site of tremendous human achievement. There were Iron Age and Romano-British settlements on the Roach Islands and presumably they used to occupy this low-lying coastal land. As the sea level rose, which it has done, very slowly, every century and is still doing at the same rate, river walls were heightened by hand labour to keep out the salt water. The Essex 'wallers' aim was to protect the land for grazing huge numbers of sheep, cattle and horses, but if they had not raised the walls, fresh water wildlife habitat would have been lost.

The Dengie Marshes and the five Roach islands were not reclaimed in one go, the walling took place over the centuries. The walls were extended one outside another, and this was particularly true on Foulness where the north end was gradually extended. The great river wall from Bradwell to Burnham, some twenty miles long, was all hand constructed by men working with shovels and barrows.

BURNHAM-ON-CROUCH

Whether you go by land or water, Burnham-on-Crouch seems to be a long way from anywhere.

The Wallet Spitway Buoy with Walton and Frinton in the background. The Spitway is a shallow channel over a sandbank and is the shortcut used as an inshore passage up the Essex coast.

The waterfront at Burnham-on-Crouch

Priors Sail Lofts, at Burnham, were built in about 1908 to store the gear from the grand yachts, during the winter.

It is about twelve miles from Burnham to the open Thames estuary at the Whitaker Spit and some Burnham yachtsmen keep their boats at Bradwell, rather than face the long beat back from the Whitaker. The attractive little town of Burnham is at the end of the road and less traffic makes it a peaceful town. The waterside has a pleasant meandering walkway weaving its way around past pubs, boatyards, chandleries and houses.

There are still pubs in Burnham, the 'Oyster Smack' on the road in, and the 'Victoria' at the other end of the town and their names just about sum up Burnham's growth, first as a centre for oyster cultivation, with a bit of barge traffic, and then blossoming into a yachting centre in the late Victorian period. When the railway came to Southminster in 1888, Burnham was transformed into a major yachting centre. When the steamer traffic had increased on the Thames it became impossible

to hold yacht races there, so the yachtsmen began to keep their yachts on the River Crouch and used to take the train up to Burnham. Men who had moved up from the Thames founded two of Burnham's four yacht clubs, the Royal Burnham and the Royal Corinthian.

John Prior, who owned the barges *George and Annie* and *Jesse* and later the *Mayland*, was a coal and oyster merchant based in a yard on the river front. In 1892 Prior bought the Buckingham Square land and built the three storey yacht repair workshop and sail storage warehouse. The Priors gradually switched over to yacht building and before World War II they were building at least one new wooden yacht every year. After the war R.J. Prior and Son resumed wooden yacht building and launched their last wooden hulled yacht, the half tonner *Harmony*, in 1980. In the 1980s, when property developers were buying up the waterfront, Priors resisted the good offers they had for

Traces of the posts, put in when the North Fambridge marshes were walled off, can still be seen. This area of grazing marsh was lost after it was flooded in 1897 when, due to the late Victorian agricultural recession, the river walls were not repaired. In about 1972 work started on digging the West Wick Marina on Stow Creek, just up the Crouch, and this was expanded in 1994.

The North Fambridge Yacht Club and new marina pontoon 2009. The last ferryman, Reg Watson, finished work in 1972, just as the moorings at North Fambridge started to increase.

their property in the middle of the Burnham waterfront. They believed in the long-term future of yacht work for themselves and their employees. In 2010 the Prior's yard was still busy with yacht repair work.

The yacht building and repair yard of William King & Son was started in about 1900 and in 1907 they built the 34ft sloop *Lona III* and carried on building yachts. They also built the Royal Burnham Yacht Club's One Designs. Herbert Page started work at the yard and later married Alice King and took over running the yard in about 1946 when they employed about thirty people. The yard closed in 1975 and then the area was cleared and houses built. It provides a pleasant place for people to live or have second homes, but without boats or life the King's Wharf has become a strangely quiet place in the middle of a lively waterfront.

Tucker Brown's boat yard was started in 1906 on land just behind the river wall. Stan Tucker left later on and started Crouch Engineering, which was taken over by his grandson Jonathan Tucker. Mike Hemingway ran Tucker Brown's yard for a while and after it closed he moved to develop the 350 berth Burnham Marina that opened, just to the west of the town, in 1988. The Burnham Museum on Coronation Street is in part of Tucker Brown's old yard.

A bold attempt to move yacht building forward was the establishment of Ferro Cement Marine Services in Station Road. I remember undertaking a yacht report for the *East Coast Digest*, a once much-loved magazine of the East Coast. The report was on the 33ft bawley yacht *Anna Crane* that had been built by Ferro Cement Services in 1976.

One September weekend I sailed on the *Anna Crane*, with her owner John Lamb and the Burnham yacht designer Alan Hill, who was constantly thinking of new ways of doing things. Alan's imaginative approach led on to him designing the 38ft ketch *Touchstone* that was built by Ferro Cement Services in 1981, for the North Fambridge cartoonist Mike Peyton. By this time fibreglass hulls had already taken over

the mass market, and put many of the small boatyards out of business. Wooden hulls were expensive, so ferro-cement seemed the cheapest option for anyone wanting to build a 'one off' hull. The *Anna Crane* was a very comfortable cruising boat, but I just did not warm to her ferro cement hull. That was irrational because ferro-cement was very practical, however within a few years there was a complete reaction against it and the Crouch's love affair with ferro faded out.

BRIDGEMARSH ISLAND

The road to Burnham runs on high ground with a wonderful view over the Crouch valley. Southend tower blocks and even ships in the Thames can be seen. This corner of Essex, from the Crouch valley to the back of Canvey, attracts London wealth. There are huge houses with their walls and imposing iron gates, the homes of people worried by the open countryside.

When coming up river one hardly notices Bridgemarsh Island, it just looks like saltings, yet it is nearly three miles long. The down river end of the back channel is known as Althorne Creek, and once had oyster cultivation grounds. When coming down the road from Althorne, past the train station, it is just possible to see the extent of Bridgemarsh Island. There were no yachts here in 1960 but then the Walker Brothers started a small boatyard, Bridgemarsh Marine here, and this has progressed to be a very smart boatyard with pontoons for yachts in Althorne Creek.

There was once a cottage on Bridgemarsh Island, and even a brick kiln, and perhaps more important it was once high yielding, wheat-growing land. In about 1921 Bridgemarsh was flooded and about 600 sheep drowned and two haystacks floated about in the river until engineers blew them up. The river didn't come over the wall, but the pressure of water washing into rabbit holes resulted in the water bursting through. In times of the agricultural depression there was little money to maintain walls for the

The 'Barge Inn' at Battlebridge.

The old mill quays are silting up at Battlebridge, at the head of the River Crouch.

The 82ft sailing barge *British Empire*, of Colchester, below the former mill at Battlebridge in 2009.

The 82ft barge *Ethel Ada* in the West Swin, a part of the channel off Foulness Island linking four mid-Essex estuaries with the Thames, across the Spitway.

long term good and it seems that Bridgemarsh was abandoned in about 1933. Most of the river walls seemed to have remained intact into the 1980s, but became badly eroded on the inside and then started to wash away.

NORTH FAMBRIDGE

There used to be a rowing ferry at North Fambridge crossing over to South Fambridge, and occasionally barges loaded straw here. In 1893 Francis B. Cooke came down from London to Burnham-on-Crouch by railway, on the Friday night 'Yachtsman's Special'. He stayed at the 'Ferry Boat Inn,' for twelve shillings a week, with his friends the Viner brothers, who had a boat there. Cooke said that the only boats at North Fambridge then were two oyster smacks and a steamboat, but he absolutely loved this remote marshland place.

In 1898 Cooke, who wrote about sailing in small boats, instigated the forming of the North Fambridge Yacht Club. A wooden shed, which

had a fascinating history, was purchased for a clubhouse. The great scandal of the Crimean War was the appalling treatment of wounded soldiers, more died in the hospitals than on the battlefields. The engineer, Brunel was asked to help come up with a solution to this problem. Within five days he had designed and ordered 500 wooden portable hospital wards. Each of these wooden wards had enough room for 28 beds. They were designed to be put up and taken down quickly, and were returned to

Britain when the war was over. One of these wooden buildings became the North Fambridge Yacht Club.

In the 1970s North Fambridge became the centre of 'build your own' ferro-cement hulls. The meadow near the 'Ferry Boat' became a land of dreams as several highly individual style hulls took shape. Wire frames were made and then the hulls were 'plastered', in one-day operations. Many dreams died in that field near the 'Ferry Boat' as people abandoned their

The Norman church of St Nicholas at Great Wakering

uncompleted hulls. 'Mick the Brick' Wilkinson, Mike Peyton gave him that name, became the chief practitioner of the ferro-cement hull building, and continued long after most people had abandoned ferro.

The marshes on the eastern shore of Stow Creek were walled off, but the river broke through and they were re-flooded by the tide. In 1974 work was started on digging out the West Wick Marina and this was expanded in 1994. After a new company took over at West Wick Marina they expanded the facilities by constructing a pontoon out into the river near the North Fambridge Yacht Club in 2006. Yachts can berth here before being taken up the shallow channel to the Marina at high water.

Seen from the air on a moonlight night the Crouch appears to be a 26 mile shaft pointing towards London and during World War I the German pilots, in both Zeppelin airships and Gotha bombers, used the river as a marker to find London. To counteract this the War Office built two airfields in 1917. The one on

Stow Marshes that was abandoned by the RAF in 1919 remains the last intact World War I airfield.

BATTLEBRIDGE

If you need furniture, Battlebridge is the place to go. The Mill Antique Centre has furniture and there is also a carpet centre nearby. There are several houseboats berthed here and this seems to have led to serious silting, but Battlebridge was once a barge port, in fact the first spritsail barge in Essex, the *Experiment*, was built here in 1791.

In 1772 Mr Battle had built a road bridge over the tidal river just below the tide mill. In 1897 W.T. Meeson closed the tide mill and opened a larger steam mill, on the north bank, just below the road bridge. The tide mill was pulled down in 1902, but the kiln and granary survived.

In 1916 another mill was built on the south quay and both mills were sold to J. & G.

Matthews, in 1926. The mill on the south side caught fire, and as the tide was out, there was no water for the fire brigade and it burnt down. When the new mill was built in 1933 a hole was dug in the river to form a reservoir in case there was another fire.

After World War II the north mill became a granary and the south mill produced 8,000tons of animal feed every year. Rankin's had two sailing barges, the *Joy* and the *Lord Roberts*, bringing imported wheat from the Royal Docks, London, up to Battlebridge and Stambridge mills. In the sailing barge days the 'hufflers'(pilots) controlled the drift of the barges in the upper Crouch reaches with a series of posts and anchors, with ropes, on the river walls to help them round corners. After these barges were sold, motor barges brought wheat up on spring tides and took freights to Yarmouth on the neap tides.

It is probable that the last motor barge up to the mill with grain was the *Peter Robin* in 1969. The mill closed in about 1985 and was pulled down, while the Granary became the antique centre. When the barges used the quay there was room for one barge to lie on the quay and another one to turn around outside her. Two Dutch barges and the wooden sailing barge *British Empire* have been permanently moored here and between 1994-2009 silting built up around them and a mud bank has started to build up in the middle of the channel.

The 82ft sailing barge *British Empire* was built by Stone Brothers at Brightlingsea in 1889 for Henry Howes, Colchester whose barges all had black tops'ls. In 1957 this barge sank off Brightlingsea laden with wheat, when owned by Francis & Gilders of Colchester. She was raised and sold to become a timber lighter at Heybridge. Later, the *British Empire* was taken to Battlebridge in an attempt to rebuild her, but that was abandoned in 2002.

WALLASEA

Wallasea Island is joined to the mainland by a road, but it can still claim to be an island because it has the River Crouch on its north side, the River Roach around the east and south and Paglesham Pool, a creek cuts inland on the landward side. Four miles long and covering some 2,200 acres, the wide-open island of Wallasea was divided into five marshland farms. These were ploughed up in World War I to produce wheat, and during the interwar agricultural depression the land went back to sheep grazing, only to be ploughed up again in World War II. Farmers say Wallasea produced about 10,000tons of wheat a year, but the urban population does not seem to see the link between farmland, and food in the supermarkets. The Government's Flooding Policy forced the farmers to give up 115 hectares on the north side to be flooded in 2006.

Since then the Flooding Policy has been extended so that the whole island could be flooded. The Roach and Crouch Harbour Authority, and boat owners from Burnham, were very worried about the negative effect of the increased flow in the river. The plan was to cover Wallasea in a metre of soil, brought in from the Olympic site in the East End of London, and London's Cross Rail. The tragedy is that this 5m tonnes of soil could have been used to make up the river walls on all the Crouch and Roach. This project, the largest in Europe, is to be achieved by taking huge sums of Government money away from coastal defences further up the East Anglian coast. It is incredible that while the Dutch are quietly raising and improving all their sea defences, the English are going to a great deal of expense to lose land on the coast and rivers.

PAGLESHAM EASTEND

The River Roach used to be called the Broomhill River, after the channel was marked with 'brooms'(withies marking the channel.) In 1848 William Kemp started boat building and was followed by Hall, who built most of the twenty-four oyster smacks that worked

The Havengore Bridge that leads to Havengore Island, at the lower end of Foulness. On the right is the Narrow Gut and to the left the Havengore Creek.

from Paglesham. Hall built the 32ft smack *Quiz* in 1872 and the 36ft *Kate* in 1883. James Shuttleworth followed Hall, and built the smacks *Our Boys* in 1911 and the 33ft *Mayfly* in 1912.

The original 'black shed' was blown down in a gale in 1881 and in its replacement James Shuttleworth built the 82ft spritsail barge *Ethel Ada* in 1903, for the Southend coal and corn merchants G & A Underwood. Frank Shuttleworth followed his father at Paglesham and built wooden yachts, and shrimpers for Leigh, until the early 1960s.

The lower end of Paglesham Pool has been used for oyster cultivation, and sailing barges used to go further up Paglesham Creek to a wharf at Church End. There had been a 'rill' (small creek) up to East Hall, that was dammed off long ago, but local farmers say that barges also went up there, behind Paglesham. The creeks leading into the rivers were the commercial highways of Victorian Essex.

The men used to load three barges with straw in a month, at Church End, and the barges returned from London with horse muck for the fields. The men were paid twenty-nine shillings a week, plus one shilling and six pence 'for a clean shirt' for unloading the muck. However in the 1920s a Paglesham man once went shopping in Woolworths and the manager asked him to leave, because the other customers were complaining that he smelt of muck!

BARLING

Many of the river walls in the Victorian era were still quite low and there was constant flooding by high tides. The marshes beside Barling Hall Creek were flooded in March 1874, and crops of beans, peas, wheat and grazing grass were destroyed.

The sailing barges *Joy* and *Lord Roberts* used to lay at anchor in the Roach, off Barlinghall Creek waiting for the high tide to get up to the mill at Stambridge. Barges used to go up above the present landing in Barlinghall Creek to load and in *Lord Roberts'* cargo books it records that part cargoes were loaded on Potton Island in 1948.

The former 'George & Dragon' on Foulness, with Churchend church in the background. The 'King's Head' at Courtsend, closed first and then the Foulness school was closed in 1988, a real indicator of a dying community. The church closed in 2007 and the 'George & Dragon' the following year.

GREAT and LITTLE WAKERING

From about 1800, locally owned sailing barges were taking farm produce up to London from the creeks between the River Roach and the coast. The area became a serious barge owning centre when Frederick and Edward Rutter of Crayford, Kent, developed brick making in Wakering. Their first brickfield was opened, in Wakering, in about 1868 and in 1874 much larger brickfields were set up at Millhead, beside Potton Creek. Another brickfield was set up at Landwick beside Havengore Creek and this was closed in about 1914. About 600 men, women and boys, were employed in the brickfields, most of whom had been recruited into the area.

The Rutters built most of their barges at Crayford and they had the reputation of being poorly built, but fast sailers. Although it was only a short passage, most of the barges went down the Crouch and through the Swin to reach the Thames, and only used Havengore as a short cut on their return trips.

Although it was only a few hours sailing, many barges were lost. The *Wakering* was run down and sunk in 1882. The *George & John* foundered, laden with bricks, at the Nore in a south-westerly hurricane in February 1894. The *Clyde*, a tiller steered barge laden with 35,00 bricks foundered near the South Shoebury buoy in a force 7 SSW gale in 1904. The *Rushley* was also loaded with bricks when she sank a mile east of Chapman Head in 1910. The *Havengore* sank near the Admiralty buoy, in 1911. The *Josephine* sank in 1912. The *Shorne* leaked so badly that she sank at a wharf in West Ham. Bricks were being taken out of Wakering in the *Anthony* and the *Gascoigne* until 1939. It was a very hard life for small deep-laden barges trading between the creeks and the Thames

MN 182 was used for dredging white weed off Shoeburyness, 2009.

wharves.

In 1945 the little 41ft spritsail barge *Cygnet* was bought for £75 and fitted with an engine and used to collect cockleshells with the fishing number HH42. The shells were collected on the Maplin Sands and taken back to Little Wakering for sale as chicken grit. An ex-army landing craft was also used to collect shells for a few years.

In 1951 E.W. 'Bill' Sutton built a 31ft wooden yacht in a barn (now demolished) behind Mortley's Nurseries at Great Wakering and had it taken down to the water in a Pickford's lorry. He teamed up with his brother-in-law Joe Wiggins and set up a boatyard in Potton Creek. The partnership built 23 wooden yachts and many other craft, although Joe Wiggins was always more interested in going out white weeding in his boat. The white weed was sorted in a yard opposite the 'Exhibition Inn.'

Bill Sutton often helped to prepare Ted Heath's yacht *Morning Cloud*, when it was racing at Burnham. Just before Bill Sutton retired he rented out a space in the yard to Steelaway to build metal hulls, and also rented space to some people who bought in a cement mixer and started building ferro-cement boats. Bill was appalled and retired to Devon and the boat yard was sold to become Wakering Boatyard.

POTTON ISLAND

The large marsh island of Potton was linked to Wakering Common by a ferry, but after the Ministry of Defence bought the island a narrow road bridge was built. The island used to be several arable farms until it got flooded in 1884. It then became grazing land until it was ploughed up when there were food shortages in World War II. Since then the land has reverted to grass and has skylarks, corn buntings and

hares.

Unfortunately the Government does not respect the Essex marsh islands and there are plans to build a nuclear waste unit on Potton and a more recent idea is to flood the island for bird habitat.

FOULNESS

Foulness is the largest of the Roach islands in south-east Essex, but seen from the sea, Foulness is just a thin line of a grass river wall on the horizon. Essex has about forty islands, some just patches of saltings but Foulness has a community in its own right. After the road bridge, into Foulness was constructed, the islands of Havengore and New England, at the southern end, have been joined together and are virtually part of Foulness.

Foulness is unique; quite different from the other places in the south-east corner of Estuary Essex. While most villages on the mainland have houses packed with ribbon developments along the roads. Foulness is spacious with a feeling, even if many of the houses are modern, that it is a survivor of the older Essex. While many nearby places are struggling to accommodate the population constantly spilling out from Greater London, Foulness has a declining population.

Foulness means 'headland of the birds' and people have lived here for a long time. There was a Romano-British settlement at Little Shelford and this lonely place seems to have been continually occupied by shepherds and fishermen. At some point the 'marsh wallers' started to put up earth walls to keep the tide out. The first record of work on sea walls was in 1271, but the island was then only about half its present size. A series of 'innings,' new walls built further out, between 1430-1833, enlarged Foulness to its present size.

The creation of walls round the marsh islands were speculative ventures by the Lords of the Manors, while the actual organization would have been paid for by the tenant farmers and the work was carried out by marsh wallers, with shovels and hand tools. Although it took centuries to achieve, these men, transformed coastal Essex into habitable land. When William Camden visited Foulness in 1607 he recorded that it was 'plentiful in grass and rich in cattle, but sheep especially' and it still is rich wheat growing farmland.

Foulness was developed as an agricultural community because of the Broomway, the road under the sea. Before the bridge was built it was only possible to reach the islands by boat at high tide, but the rest of the time the muddy creeks were impossible to cross. Someone had the idea of making a road, the Broomway, out on the Maplin Sands, which could be used at low tide. This was a five-mile track over the sands from Wakering Stairs along the south-eastern side of the island, with tracks going off to different farms on Foulness. The track on the sands was marked with posts, with brooms on the top. In

The RNLI lifeboat crew at Southend with their hovercraft, 2010. The RNLI at Southend have a hovercraft on the landward end of the pier, for going on the flats at low tide and also have an inshore lifeboat. At low tide they use another lifeboat kept at the end of the pier.

old Essex speech, a 'mapple' was a small mop made of broom, and it is thought that the name Maplin Sands derives from those early markers.

At the northern end of the Broomway a track leads off to Fisherman's Head and then over the wall to the small village of Courtsend. Fishermen's Head was also the site of the Kettle, or on Foulness 'Keddel,' the fish trap. The early medieval fish traps on the Blackwater in Goldhanger creek, were made of wicker, and there were others at East Mersea and Bradwell. The traps on Foulness were nets on posts, in a v shape, so that the fish were driven into them and retrieved at low tide. The fish traps at Fisherman's Head were still being worked in the early 1940s and were the last ones used on the East Coast.

The Broomway first appears in the records of the Bailiff of Great Wakering in 1419. There are many tales of carts getting stuck out on the Maplins. The carters used to leave the carts and gallop off on their horses for the higher ground as the tide, whipped up by a strong winds, came roaring across the sands earlier than expected. The Broomway is still a public right of way, but it is best used with a local guide. It is no longer marked and going on the sands, with pools, rills and linns, can be very dangerous. The sands are also used as an MOD firing range, mostly between Mondays and Fridays, and must be avoided when there are red flags flying.

The War Department first established the artillery firing range on the mainland at Shoeburyness in 1855. The War Department purchased Foulness, under the title 'Lord of the Islands,' in 1915 and closed it to the general public, and it has remained closed ever since.

The population of Foulness was quite low when it was just used for sheep and cattle grazing. It was then a remote place only visited by cattle dealers. When prize fighting was outlawed Foulness was one of the Essex

Low tide at Southend Pier.

marshes that the 'sporting gentry' flocked to for the big fights. The demand for food in the Napoleonic War saw the marshes come under the plough and more people were needed for arable farming.

In 1871 Foulness had a population of 754 people, all relying on the Broomway for contact with the outside world. In 1922 the Government built the military road and first bridge, which had to be opened so that the brick barges could go through. In the 1953 Floods the whole of Foulness was under water. Amazingly no one was drowned on Foulness, but for two days the people watched from their bedrooms as the cattle were being drowned out on the grazing marshes. Eventually a fleet of little boats arrived and took them to the reception centres at Burnham.

In 1988 a new opening bridge was built, but mechanized farming required less labour and work on the firing range declined and by 1961 the population was down to 316. People remain fiercely loyal to their Foulness roots and on the 'Open Days,' at the Foulness Heritage Centre, they still return to reminisce. By 2010 there were twenty-four empty houses on Foulness and the population was believed to be below 145. Having to go past the guard at Landwick Gate does not deter people from living on Foulness, and some commute to jobs off the

island. However if you want to own your house you have to move to mainland Essex.

Foulness still has a Post Office, that is something, and one can't help admiring the people who have determinedly gone on living on this marsh island, but apart from the occasion explosions, it is a very peaceful place.

THORPE BAY

Thorpe Bay is to the west of Shoeburyness and is regarded as being the smart end of Southend-on-Sea. There are large houses, in a slight bay on the seafront, overlooking a green. For much of the time the water of the Thames Estuary is a very long way away across mud flats. Thorpe Bay is a very well organized seaside commuter town with well-painted beach huts, and an orderly and popular yacht club with small yachts lying on moorings on the Southend Flats.

SOUTHEND-ON-SEA

Southend was the South End of the older settlement of Prittlewell. In the Anglo-Saxon period Prittlewell was an important place. A formal burial, possibly of a prince of the East Saxons, was found when a road was widened. There was a later royal connection when the Prince Regent arranged for his Princess Caroline to stay in the Royal Terrace. Lord

The steel sailing barge *Decima* ghosting along in the Southend barge race. The *Decima* was built for Goldsmiths, of Grays, who had 120 barges before World War I, the largest fleet of sailing barge.

Nelson also stayed at this new watering place.

In the early nineteenth century Southend started as a resort for the smart London society, but when the railway line was constructed through the town to Shoeburyness, this quickly changed and it became a great favourite with the East Enders. The name of Southend-on-Sea was given so that people in London were aware that it was a seaside resort.

Southend still has many of the handsome buildings of the early Victorian period, but the huge twentieth century high-rise buildings, that tower above, giving wonderful views out over the busy estuary, over shadow these. Southend has its own strong character, and is more like a small northern American city than the other Essex resorts further up the coast.

Southend's popularity as being 'London-by-the-Sea' was mainly due to the beach on the sea front. However Southend entrepreneurs were brilliant at providing entertainment for trippers, and when the sea recedes away from the beach the lack of sea for bathing is not noticed. The building of Southend Pier started in 1828, and over the years grew to become the longest in the world, at two and half miles long.

The new pier was not popular with the local barge owners, the Vandervords, who used to load their barges, on the open beach, with farm produce destined for London. Abraham Vandervord had three barges, *Royal Oak, Minerva* and *Waterloo* running a hoy service between Southend, which was then an Essex village similar to Maldon, and the Upper Pickled Herring Wharf in London. The Vandervords supported the building of the Pier, but were furious when they were charged to land their barges on the open beach. In 1834 when the company collector boarded the barge *Minerva,* John Vandervord threatened to shoot him, and his brother George threatened to knock him overboard with the windlass handspike. Three days later, when there was an attempt to collect tolls from the *Royal Oak,* the watermen, presumably under the Vandervords instructions, broke the pier tollgate down. After this the Wickford Magistrates fined the Vandervords for non-payment.

The Vandervords tried to get out of paying dues by landing their barges at Shoeburyness, but this was within three miles of the Pier so they still had to pay. In the 1870s the 'fighting Vandervords' were still battling with the Local Board (Council) over charges for unloading barges. The last Vandervord sold his business to Goldsmiths of Grays in 1900 and sold his last barge, the *Jane*, in about 1913. Barges continued to use the Jetty at Southend, and the last Southend owned sailing barge, the *Ashingdon* was sold in 1952.

By the late Victorian period huge numbers of trippers were coming to Southend and this created a demand for pleasure trips in boats. The beach was divided into 'pitches' that were jealously guarded, and there was deep rivalry between the East and West Beaches. Yarmouth yawls were bought, second hand, and were converted to pleasure boats. Heywood came from Deal in 1886 and built the yawl *Skylark*, on Southchurch beach, for the Lilly Brothers. This was followed by the *Jubilee* for George and Alfred Myall. These yawls where used for 'stowboating' for sprat and one winter, Joe Myall's yawl *Conqueror* was run down by a steamer while fishing.

The pleasure yawls carried a good spread of sail and the larger boats took trippers down to the Nore lightship or across to Sheerness, for a shilling (5p) a head,. The pleasure yawls and local fishing bawleys lay on moorings off the beach. At the height of summer, when the yawls couldn't cope with the demand, bawleys were also used to carry passengers. The fish holds were scrubbed out and deck chairs put down there for passengers to sit on if it rained.

Southend Pier proved useful for the fishermen to land their fish when the tide was down and the pier created shelter from the southwest wind. It is the Londoners great love of shellfish and shrimps that has kept the local fishing fleets alive at the Thames mouth. The Southend and Leigh fishermen were deadly rivals but they both used 'bawleys.' Shrimps were cooked as soon as they came out of the water, which improved the taste. To achieve this, 'coppers' with a fire underneath were fitted on boats in about 1840. These boats were known as 'boiler boats,' corrupted into bawley, and were wider than the normal fishing smacks so that the boiling water did not spilt on the way home.

As well as tripper boats Heywood built cocklers at the Vulcan Works near the Kursaal. When the Leigh men came to look at a new boat they came 'mob handed' in case there was any trouble with the Southend fishermen. Bill Heywood had a steam traction engine which towed new boats, such as the cocklers *Mary Amelia* and *Reindeer*, built in 1914, out on to the sands at low tide and as the tide came up they floated off. During World War I, Cochran became Heywood's partner, and after the war they bought an old army tank to tow craft out on to the sands.

Even when engines were fitted, fishermen still preferred the shallow draft, transom sterned, bawley type of hull. Southend was the centre of whitbait fishing in the Thames Estuary and Young Bros of Southend had the 34ft motor bawley *Saxonia*, built in 1932, for whitebaiting. In World War II the *Saxonia* worked out of Holehaven, and her elderly skipper used to get a lift over, in an army lorry, every morning, but his daughter, who was acting as his mate, had to cycle over. The Youngs were pair- boat fishing for whitebait until 1966, when the Larsen trawling, and freezing, took over.

The Thomas family owned most of the bawleys at Southend, and Cook of Maldon built the last one, the 38ft *Souvenir*, for S. Thomas in 1933. By 2010 only two steel fishing boats, owned by the Gilsons, were being kept on the sands at Southend.

The end of Southend Pier does not sound like the sort of place that was ever important, but it was vital during World War II. In spite of very heavy bombing the Port of London never closed and to keep shipping flowing, convoys were organized from the end of Southend Pier. Ships anchored here and waited for their instructions to sail under naval protection. Between September 1939, and June 1945, over 3000 convoys were assembled at the Thames mouth. In those three thousand convoys there were about 84,000 ships.

OLD LEIGH

The commuter town of Leigh-on-Sea is a network of streets on the high ground over looking the Thames Estuary. Old Leigh is the fishing and tourist village at the foot of the cliff, sandwiched between the railway line and the open estuary. Old Leigh has something for everyone. This is a place with 'character' and people are drawn here during summer weekends, when the pubs and restaurants on the little street are packed. There is a beach at the far end of the narrow street. This always had some sand, but has been much improved by the delivery of eight lorry loads of golden yellow sand.

In the nineteenth century, as the Thames became more polluted, the centre of fishing moved down river toward the mouth. As Old Leigh had clean water, and a railway link, it thrived as a fishing centre. However the waterfront is only accessible by boat at high tide. The Gut, a narrow channel, twists its way through the mud flats from Old Leigh to the Ray Gut and on into the Thames mouth. Even thought there are small navigation buoys, it is difficult for a decked craft to navigate this without local knowledge, however it is regularly used by Leigh's flourishing fishing fleet.

One of Old Leigh's pubs, the 'Peter Boat,' takes its name from the boats originally used here. These boats probably had their origins in the Anglo-Saxon craft of fifteen hundred years ago. They were open, clinker-built, double ended (a point at each end) boats and had a simple spritsail rig. The Peter Boats were suitable for working in creeks and making coastal passages in fine weather. The next stage had been a 'pinkie,' a slightly larger decked craft and they were followed by the 'bawley,' for which Leigh became famous.

Although Leigh had a large fleet of fishing craft, very few were actually built here. Cann's of Harwich built some of the best sailing bawleys, such as the 42ft *Maud* and the 40ft *Doris*. When engines came in, the Leigh men had similar craft built, with less draft, and it appears that the *Alpha* was the last one built, in 1938.

The Leigh sailing cocklers sailed out at high water and ran ashore on the sandbanks in the Thames Estuary, usually on the Maplins, and at low water the crew hand raked the cockles out of the sands. The 35ft *Mary Amelia* loaded 265 baskets of cockles, at fifty to a ton in the winter, and forty in the summer. The men did the raking and boys carried the baskets back to the cockler. The 'Governor' (skipper) walked around the sands looking for better places to find cockles on the next trip.

Once the cocklers were loaded the men slept, and had a cup of tea before the cockler floated, and they hauled the boat off the bank on their anchor and sailed for Leigh. On a good day they were loaded down to one plank below the deck. On the motor cocklers there were often as many as thirteen men aboard. On their return trip some of the men used to play cards in the forepeak. If they had lost their days earnings at cards, some men used to jump off at the last bend in the Gut to avoid the heavy work of unloading the cockles.

The 36ft cockler *Endeavour*, built at the Strand Wharf, Leigh, by Cole & Wiggins in 1924, was one of the new type of motor cockler, but they still had sails to help the low powered engine along and used the centreboard to stop them rolling. In 1940 the *Endeavour* was one of six cocklers ordered to Dunkirk for the Evacuation of the British Army. On the way back to Leigh the Osborne's cockler *Renown*, was being towed by *Letitia*, when a mine blew her up and all four

Five loaded barges at Bell's Wharf, Old Leigh, 1928. They were bringing in bricks and cement from Kent and imported timber from the Surrey Docks for the boom in house building.

The sailing barge *Regard* at Bell's Wharf, Old Leigh, 1928.

The sailing cocklers *Alice & Florrie* and *Mary Amelia* lying between Bell's and Theobold's wharves at the 4th Leigh Fishing Festival, in 2009.

The 36ft Leigh bawley *Helen & Violet* was built by Canns at Harwich in 1906 for shrimp fishing from Leigh. She had a shrimp boiling copper in her for her first thirty years.

men aboard were killed. As a memorial to these men, Brian Kennel and Shaun White rebuilt the *Endeavour* for the Endeavour Trust in 2005.

The old style of hand-raking cockles ended after the Meddle family were allowed to try using a suction dredger on the *Ranger II* in 1967. The wooden boats have been replaced by the steel flat-bottomed suction dredgers that hoover up the cockles from the sands at high tide. However, cockling is very closely controlled to a set number of boats, and the number of days they can work.

Leigh also became the centre for white weeding, one of the Thames Estuary's most curious fisheries. White weed is a type of coral that grows in sheltered parts of the seabed and is dredged up and sold as decoration. In about 1948 the demand for white weed caused many Essex boats to switch from fishing to dragging rakes along the seabed for white weed. By the early 1950s there was a kind of gold rush and at least one man sold his house to buy a boat

to go white weeding. By 1994 the number of boats white weeding had dropped to twenty-four. When plastic decorations came in, there were no boats operating rakes, but in a greener age, natural products were in demand again, for funeral wreaths made of white weed, and this provided work for three boats.

Leigh had been a port and sailing barges were owned here from the late eighteenth century. Joe Deal was the last pilot to take small coasters up to both Leigh and Southend. The last one he took to Theobald's Wharf, Leigh, was the coaster *Georgina* in 1982.

To the east of Old Leigh is the Essex Yacht Club's clubhouse, the ex-Royal Navy experimental fibreglass minesweeper, *HMS Wilton*. In 2009, 112 people were trapped aboard the minesweeper when she moved during their Christmas Lunch and the gangway was lost. The Fire Fighters came to the rescue and got everyone ashore safely.

The bridge over the railway near *HMS Wilton*

The Leigh cocklers in 2006. There were only thirteen boats licensed to suction dredge for cockles in the Port of London area of the Thames Estuary and they are highly restricted to how many cockles can be landed. The restrictions prevent the cockle stock from being exhausted.

Osborne Bros shellfish stall, outside the 'Crooked Billet, Old Leigh.

is called the Gypsy Bridge and the channel across the mud flats to the main channel is the Gypsy Gut. These were named after the clipper bowed schooner yacht *Gypsy*, built in New York in 1850, which was the Essex Yacht Club's first clubhouse.

TWO TREE ISLAND

The 170 acre Two Tree Island does not quite live up to its name. There were two elm trees here, but they blew down in a storm in about 1965, probably after being killed by the 1953 Flood.

Originally there were two cattle grazing islands, now joined into one. On the East side was Oxfleet, while the western end was Haughess. Each island had a causeway connected to the mainland. This marsh island became linked to the mainland with a road-bridge so that rubbish could be brought in and dumped but this was stopped and the island has become a nature reserve with two public car parks. A watch is now kept during the nesting season, because an egg collector stole avocet eggs one year.

Canvey appears to have been the first place in Essex to be developed as an area for people from the East End of London to escape, to find fresh air and peace. Chalet villages were built on Canvey early in the twentieth century. By 1914 there were 600 people living on Canvey and in 1947 the population had risen to 10,030. It was still rising when disaster struck, on the night of the East Coast Floods, on January 30, 1953. A huge surge tide roared down the east of England over topping the river walls and sea defences. Canvey was the worst hit place on the East Coast. About fifty-eight people were drowned and the entire population of 11,500 people were made homeless. The Government announced that after the 1953 Floods no more homes were to be built on land below sea level. In fact within thirty years the number of homes below sea level had more than doubled and by 1981 Canvey alone had a population of over 35,000. In the heavily populated area of southern England space for people is in short supply, so that every piece of low-lying land is vital in our overcrowded island.

CANVEY ISLAND

Canvey lies at the entrance to the River Thames and is only about twenty-six miles from the centre of London and five from Southend-on-Sea. The island seems to have been a remote marsh, grazed by sheep until about 1637, when the young Dutchman, Cornelius Vermuyden agreed to wall the island off from tidal water. When the work was finished, about 200 of Vermuyden's Dutch workers, the 'Low Country Strangers,' settled on Canvey and began to farm the land they had reclaimed.

Robert Simper sailed in some of the last barges trading under sail. When he was nineteen he sailed across the North Sea in his own gaff cutter *Sea Fever*. In 1963 he was one of the people who started the Old Gaffers Association and went on to be East Coast President and national President of the OGA. He has been Chairman of the Sutton Hoo Society and is Commodore of the Bawdsey Haven Yacht Club. He was chairman of the Dawn Sailing Barge Trust when the barge *Dawn* was being rebuilt at Heybridge and is a Director of the Cambria Trust that has rebuilt the barge *Cambria*.

He has had 37 books published, mostly about the East Coast. Has written a feature in the magazine *Sea Breezes* for forty-four years and many features for *Classic Boat* and many other magazines. In 2010 the World Ship Trust awarded him a citation 'for many years of helping to record and preserve so much of the country's vintage sailing craft.'

He has been married to Pearl for fifty-two years and has three children and six grandchildren.